MOMFIDENT
As F*ck

by

Courtney St. Croix

Copyright © 2020 Courtney St Croix/MOMFIDENT AF Media

All rights reserved. No part of this book may be reproduced, scanned, or distributed in any printed or electronic form without permission.

Cover Design - Christina Williams
Cover and Author Photo - Ashley Adams
Interior - Courtney St Croix

ISBN: 978-1-7770177-0-5

For more information, visit www.GetMomfidentAF.com
or email hello@momfidentaf.com

This book is dedicated to any mama who needs encouragement, support, love and care from those around her, and who often second-guesses her awesome-ness despite being a f*cking amazing, incredible, worthy and capable woman, inside and out.

So, like, every mom ever.

Table of Contents

Introduction - NICE TO MEET YOU! *Waves*	1
Chapter One - Entering The Mother-Hood	10
Chapter Two - A Brief History of "Momfident As F*ck"	23
Chapter Three - Body Language	35
Chapter Four - Effective Handling of Changing Bods	45
Chapter Five - Accepting Your Now	55
Chapter Six - Getting Confident (AF)	64
Chapter Seven - Mindset Shifts. They're Like, So Fetch.	72
Chapter Eight - Assessing Pivotal Moments	86
Chapter Nine - Unicorn Self-Love Assistants	95
Chapter Ten - Movement Matters	102
Chapter Eleven - Yoga Sch-Moga	122
Chapter Twelve - Body Image and Stuff	130
Chapter Thirteen - Tamagotchs, Diversity, Conformity, and Confidence	145
Chapter Fourteen - Anti-Social Media	164
Chapter Fifteen - Making Mom-nections	179
Chapter Sixteen - Navigating Mom-Guilt	189
Chapter Seventeen - Rose Coloured Self-Image	205
Last Word	219

Introduction

NICE TO MEET YOU! *WAVES*

Hey friend. How's your day going? It must be a relatively good day so far, if you've found five minutes of your own to sit down, crack open a book—gasp—and start reading with every intention of digging in and finishing in a reasonable amount of time, right? (HA! Reasonable. Forget reasonable and just try to read a page every day. If it takes you eight months to read every page, I'm not offended. Thanks for being here.)

First thing's first: a massive and sincere thank you for grabbing a copy of my book! I'm just a regular mom[3] like you, and I'm guessing if this book caught your eye, you're looking for some help in the confidence, self, and body-love department. Say no more. While nothing in these pages reinvents the wheel, it's a collection of relevant mom-specific-topics, experiences, and stories

---

3 (*But actually I'm not a regular mom, I'm a cool mom.)

from my own personal journey that I hope will help generate your own perspectives of how you see yourself operating in this perfection-driven world.

Let me ask you something—er, a few things. Do you have trouble strutting your stuff like America's Next Top Mom-Model as you walk proudly from your beach chair to the water sans towel? Do you struggle with comparing your own body, life, and circumstances with other moms, the ones you see on social media or the ones you see at Starbucks whose kids seem to behave all the time and who never seem to have a stained shirt or unkempt hair? Do you have a hard time accepting your postpartum body? Do you have a poor body image due to years and years of negative self-talk and judgement, even if others tell you you're crazy? Do you constantly start and then "fall off" of diets, workout plans, and buy any product that claims you can "lose weight fast" because you just want to feel good about your figure again? Do you suffer from feelings of mom-guilt every time you dare to crave some alone time, or just wanna be able to go to the DAMN BATHROOM ALONE FOR FIVE MINUTES, IS THAT TOO MUCH TO ASK?!?!?! Yeah, I thought so. Me too. While I can't patch all the holes in your life, and while there is much work to be done in terms of mindset and behavioural changes to help you feel satisfied and fulfilled in all aspects of your mom-life, more than anything, this book will be a companion for you, a friend, a confidant. I want this book to remind you, any time you need it, that you're abso-fucking-lutely not alone in your quest to somehow find a way to be happy with yourself as you are, right now. Know that you will experience struggle as you attempt to do so. Know that anyone who prioritizes healing the relationship with themselves (that's you, mama!) straps in for the long haul and respected the process, myself included. I know you can get there, and with a little (hopefully) well-worded experience dropping and maybe a few strategically placed f-bombs, we should really make some good progress with the stories inside these pages. I also know that the water is muddied slightly by the fact that you probably have a kid, or two, or four, and it isn't all rainbows and sunshine and flicking a switch to self-love the moment you read the intro of a new book. I get that you have multiple thoughts in your head at all times. I get that you're overwhelmed and stressed and are trying to remember everything for everybody, yourself included. I get that you can't always have a perfect and organized morning routine to start your day. I get that you can't even have a hot coffee to yourself on most days. Probably, most importantly, I get that you're not only struggling to manage your own self and your own thoughts, but also: get to the gym, eat well, drink your green juice, take your vitamins, journal for 6 hours a day, do yoga, be grateful, pick-up the dry cleaning, get the groceries, excel in your career, clean the house, do the laundry, answer everybody's text messages, RSVP to four birthday parties, make cupcakes for the school bake sale… OH, and don't forget, also oversee and be heavily responsible for the behaviour, schedules, manners, development, emotions and school lunches of several unequipped, emotionally unstable, slow-as-molasses tiny humans.

Yeah, I'm not gonna give you a blueprint for how many days a week to workout, how to incorporate gratitude into your morning routine, or give you a magical solution that will reduce all the stress, anxiety, overwhelm, and insecurities in your life. (It's probably essential oils though, right? They fix everything.) I know you. I get you. I understand you. And I hope that means you will feel seen, heard, and supported as you read through some of my "advice." I'm just like you. *Fist bump* Let's do this.

Okay, so, who am I anyway? What makes me qualified to tell you how to live a more confident mom life? A mom life so confident it can only be measured with the unit "As F*ck"?

Well, nothing really. Like I said, I'm just a regular person like you. If you ever see me in the street or at Starbucks, please say hello to me! I am just a passionate woman who wants to share everything I have learned on my own path to healing my negative self-image. I want to help other women learn how to do the same thing. I also hope that your own perspective and mindset shifts will have a positive influence on your children as they see your actions, notice, and follow suit in their own way (because you know they're always watching, #amIright). I'm sharing my top strategies that I work on with my group and private clients of mindset coaching. For the most part, it's just the best pieces of a trial-and-error period of about five years of my life, where I not only began to acknowledge the negative bull-crap I was regularly thinking about myself (shit-thinking, but we'll get to that later), but started to make a change so I no longer automatically believed it or allowed it to define me in any way. I'm on a journey that I believe is ongoing, never-ending, and BTW, totally worth the long-term effort and focus. I promise. This may be your first step or your hundredth, but there will always be more steps available to tackle, and you might even step down a few before you go back up again. That's totes cool.

So that we're properly introduced, hi! *Waves* I'm Courtney. I'm an entrepreneur, wife to my high school sweetheart, mom to a sassy four-year-old named Presley, life-long-student, fitness instructor, author, producer, and confidence coach. I enjoy writing, dancing, sarcasm, and chocolate chip cookies, but not beer or vanilla ice cream. Ew. I would love to know more about you, too! Pause for a quick sec and find me on Instagram (@momfidentaf). Send me a DM and say "Hi, I'm _____" and give me the Coles notes on you, too. There, now it's a real convo! Okay, back to the book.

Still "qualification" curious? Okay, well, I am trained as a Life Coach specializing in Women's Confidence and Life Purpose, and I have been coaching women on confidence and self-esteem in multiple different settings for nearly fifteen years. I am the host and producer of my top-rated show, "The Momfidence Podcast" that serves many women and moms on their journey, and I created a signature #MOMFIDENTAF Self-Love journal after noticing how beneficial journalling was to my process of becoming a more confident version of me. I have an online self-study course called *"Love Your #MomBod NOW!"* and I co-created an online fitness program (with @keepfit.women) especially for busy moms, so I can continue to support healthy living and share my passion for body diversity and representation in the fitness industry. I have a bachelor's degree in English Literature from the University of Toronto and I have several Life Coaching and Leadership Certifications. My biggest qualification is probably this: my desire to help women like you. I don't believe that you need necessarily to acquire growth and learning from only someone with a PhD in psychology, but if you do, I'm not offended. This just maybe isn't the book for you. I'm not here to call myself an expert or guru on mom-confidence, but I have definitely learned a few things that I feel will be helpful if passed on, and I'm all about sharing the love. And I want to let you in on a little secret: there aren't any author police. If you want to write a book because you know your message has the power to help people, GO. FOR. IT. Seriously! We might as well do the whole disclaimer thing now while we're here: the things you'll hear in this book are my story and my opinions only. During my career in fitness, I noticed a sad (and wide) gap between how the average woman views her exterior body and how she subsequently links her value and worth so closely to it, so I decided to start a conversation about self-acceptance in a climate that forces women to think they aren't good enough if they aren't a specific size and weight. Nothing in this book should be taken as a replacement for seeking medical assistance from your healthcare professional, especially if you find your feelings of insecurity and lack of confidence are far deeper than just loathing your stretch marks and wanting to lose weight to feel better about yourself. So *DISCLAIMER ALERT* this book is my opinion and my opinion only.

If you've enjoyed anything I've said thus far, you'll probably like the realizations, support, suggestions and stories in this book that are pulled mostly from my own personal experience. If you prefer your authors to have heaps of scholarly credentials, doctorate degrees or a slew of academic awards... *shrugs* that ain't me, sis. I *did* get the geography award in elementary school, though, and I was valedictorian in the eighth grade so... I know. Impressive. Doesn't that *technically* make me an "award-winning" author? HA! Get ready for a lot more of those kind of sarcastic, history-referencing zingers, because there's a lot of 'em coming your way. I'm 1000% okay with the credentials that I do have, and I believe we can find acceptance and forward motion through the power of conversation and connection. You and me, we're connected and we're conversing. Right now. Look at us! I believe it isn't always about the credentials, and that you and I can connect and improve ourselves together, based on the shared experience of struggle in both life and confidence-level. I also like to think that by leading the way and showing you that if me, a normal AF person (just like you) can go ahead and *write a damn book*, then you, too, can do just about whatever the fuck you want babe, even learn how to love your current self, the one that exists right now, as you're reading this. Yes, you can! Love your bod, dye your hair purple, write your own book, start a podcast, or go for that promotion. Even rock the crap out of your bathing suit even though you don't have a perfect body! We can do this, sis.

I'm not a doctor, I don't have a PhD, and I'm not

going to force you to listen to me. Take this book for what you will; take the best pieces and leave anything that doesn't resonate with you. Use it to help you during difficult days, and share it with a friend if you find it makes a difference in your life. I hope you find it helpful.

We're just two normal, average human beings, you and me. Maybe you're a mom, maybe you're not. (I only mention this because despite the title of this book and the fact that my focus is generally on moms, many of my clients and community members are not yet moms but find my perspectives and stories helpful nonetheless. So if you haven't squeezed a watermelon-sized human out of your body in some way, that's okay. You're welcome here!)

So sit down with a glass of wine, or a coffee or tea, or even a huge jug of water, and let this information seep into your body and mind like a nice warm bath. Let my words spread over you like a bath bomb fizzing away in that hot water, and absorb everything you can from this book so you can take a more confident step forward tomorrow, and the next day, and the next.

This is a journey, and it's about slow progress. Just like fitness. You don't change your body in one day, and you don't change your mind in one day either. Commit to feeling a little bit better about yourself every day, and you're already winning.

Chapter One
ENTERING THE MOTHER-HOOD

Let's just collectively agree on the following statement right now, before we go anywhere. Becoming a mom for the first time may be most accurately described in one single word: Hard. Scratch that, actually, it's two words: **Fucking hard.**

Pregnancy is hard, labour is hard, delivery is hard, newborns are hard, getting no sleep is hard, hormonal emotions are hard, postpartum breasts are, literally, hard (and painful,) babies are hard, toddlers, kids, teenagers, young adults, various stages... hard. Mother-fucking h-a-r-d. Even conceiving one of these little miracles can be hard. Agreed? Okay cool. We have this in common. Look at us, bonding!

And all of that, coupled with the sleepless nights,

overwhelm, hormones, conflicting advice, and "I-don't-know-what-the-eff-I'm-doing" syndrome, can make it difficult to find yourself, your health, and your confidence after entering this mother-hood. Not to mention your old bod, what a shit-show that poor girl has been through, am I right?

I experienced all of the aforementioned symptoms of new motherhood, and even though I live quite a fit and active lifestyle, I still had a hell of a time trying to get my "pre-pregnancy" body back in tip top shape. And contrary to popular belief, one does not have all the glorious time in the world while struggling through that first year of mom-dom, to get her ass back into the gym and #workitout, as this damn society may make us believe. And I know, some moms have it easier, with unicorn babies who sleep 7 hours at a time as soon as they're 3 days old, but let me tell ya, that did NOT happen to me.

("And another thing!" *Raises finger*)

Even when attempting tried and true weight loss, fitness and nutrition programs, that had worked for me in the past, I couldn't quiiiiite get back the old pre-pregs bod I was longing for. I wasn't "bouncing back" like I had hoped and expected. I wasn't bouncing anywhere, to be honest. Shit is just different now. *Shrugs*

The problem was, I had a hard expectation that I would just immediately go back to being the same ~~person~~ body I was before. My expectations needed to be adjusted. And, listen, we all have different bodies. Your body is different from mine, and our bods are different from every other woman. I also would like to mention that the body I had pre-pregnancy was not necessarily one that I was overtly happy with anyway. I'm not sure why there was a massive priority cloud over getting "that" body back, when I was never even appreciative or happy with it to begin with. But I digress.

Maybe you're reading this, and you're like, "Well, *I've* been 115 pounds since college and I'm still 115 pounds after having kids. So, what *now*, Courtney?" Well, to that I would say: AMAZING! All body sizes, weights, and shapes are amazing and accepted here in this space. I would argue, though, that you *are* a different woman than you were in college, even if your body still looks the same on the outside. And perhaps you're looking for a different kind of confidence, other than body confidence. That's cool, babe. If you're here to get sorted out and improve your overall confidence, even if you feel pretty good about your body already, you can still benefit from some of the techniques that will follow. I'm sure of it!

My guess would be, that even though your weight specifically may be a non-issue, that you have insecurities of your own. They are different from mine. They come from different places, for different reasons. But the reality is that we all have insecurities about something. Which is unfortunate, but true. Women are generally extremely hard on themselves. *Raises hand* I know I was. I spent an insurmountable amount of energy agonizing over the smallest little details that nobody would ever notice, let alone think twice about. Could anyone tell I'd gained a few pounds? Was someone noticing the cellulite on the back of my legs? Is my belly pooch showing through this shirt? Does it show at this angle? It does, doesn't it? DAMMIT.

It's an unfortunate reality that many women judge ourselves too harshly, are ridiculously critical of ourselves and our appearance, allow our weight and our size to dictate our value and our worth as human beings, compare ourselves to other women and to basically every (skewed) marketing image we see before us, and generally have a soundtrack of terrible negative self-talk playing on repeat no matter how hard we try to be better, fitter, stronger. Well, it's an unfortunate reality in the *Western* world, anyway. There are plenty of places around the world where women do not see themselves against other women's shapes, sizes, or abilities, nor do they validate themselves based on their aesthetic or having certain "things." They simply see themselves for themselves and for their strengths. They see themselves as people of the earth, and just like all trees and flowers don't perfectly resemble one-another, they understand that humans shouldn't, either. I plan to take a cue from these women. I hope you'll join me.

North America (et al) has it really ass-backwards. We perceive the world as having specific "types" and specific "looks" and those are the accepted molds we must fit into, so that we fit in accordingly. We perceive that we always need to look better, skinnier, fitter; have longer hair, eyelashes, and thicker eyebrows (but of course, to not have any other hair other than that...); to be prettier, have bigger lips, bigger boobs, smaller waists, and to have specific and sometimes expensive "things" in order to fit in. This, of course, is the entire women's advertising industry in a nutshell. It screams, "YOU ARE NOT GOOD ENOUGH" followed by, "YOU SHOULD BUY THIS PRODUCT TO FEEL YOU ARE." And it works. Too many times. Hasn't it worked on you?

Haven't you picked up an anti-wrinkle cream to make sure your skin doesn't age too quickly? Haven't you succumbed to a hot new diet trend that includes some magic shakes, pills, supplements or other products that promise you can lose 20 pounds in 20 days? Haven't you dyed your hair, or gotten eyelash extensions, or used a self-tanner, or bought the Spanx, or micro-bladed your brows, or purchased the cellulite cream?

I am not asking these things to judge you. Let's make that abundantly clear. I'm asking you so we can relate to one another. I've done every single one of those things listed above. I've spent years of my life agonizing over how I look, what I weigh, how I could look skinnier, and spot reduce, and melt fat, and weigh less, and slim down, and shape up, and be wrinkle-free, and not appear fat to anybody, *especially* other people. And I'm telling you right now, those years were spent wasting my valuable energy. They blocked me from just focusing on living life. They stopped me from having delicious foods at potlucks, hanging out with my friends during the most social time of my life, avoiding being in group photos, and not enjoying myself or participating in activities while on vacation because I "felt fat" in my bathing suit. And I don't want that for you, sister. Not anymore.

I've fallen prey to many of these marketing strategies, over and over and over again. It all stems from the comparison concept. Maybe this will land with you too. Everything I have in my makeup drawer is fine, but then I see an advertisement of a beautiful, thin model who looks perfect (and is photoshopped and edited by the best in the business), and is wearing some new shade of the exact same lip gloss, and suddenly I have to have it. It makes an unspoken promise that I can have her life, if I get that lip gloss. It's why we go into Sephora for beach hair spray, and leave with $327 worth of stuff we don't need and didn't intend on buying.

They've got us. It's high time we break that cycle. Take a moment of pause and reflection here, mama. Close your eyes, and take a few deep breaths, then open up and read this part carefully:

Look down at yourself and your body, wherever you are. Put one hand on your body somewhere. **Pay close attention to these words.**

This is your body. It's the only body you have. It's your reality, right now.

This body has served you well. It's gotten you to this very moment, this exact point in time, in your life, in your existence.

This body houses every single memory and experience you've had in your life; it's taken you on trips, it's met other incredible people, it's supported friends in times of need, and it's been supported by others during your own difficult times.

This body has provided you a tiny human or two. It has miraculously grown entirely new people and birthed them into this world. I think we forget about this sometimes... but creating, growing, and birthing a baby is literally a miracle on earth. Just a reminder.

This body was not created to be perfect, or fit into a pre-determined "box", or look just like anybody else.

This is the only body you have, and it's time to condition her with love, instead of hate.

This body is only one part, one teeny, tiny percentage of an incredible human being that lives and breathes inside these bones. This body deserves respect and acceptance. Right now.

Skin has been stretched. Uteruses have been maxed out. Pounds have been put on. Shape has been tested. Comments have been made. ("Oh my gosh, you're so big, is it twins? You must be due any day now!" Actually, random stranger in the grocery store line, it isn't twins, and actually, I am only 30 weeks today. But thanks for making me question my pregnant-body confidence YET AGAIN.)

A PERSON/PEOPLE HAVE BEEN CARRIED INSIDE OF YOU. So, yeah, it's different. Give your bod a break, will ya? She deserves it. What I struggled with, as we all seem to do in this new world of constant comparison, was the fact that my body didn't look exactly like it did before I got pregnant. EXACTLY. That's what my expectation was. *Exact.*

For months, I agonized over the fact that I *still* wasn't back to my pre-pregnancy weight. I exercised, I ate nutritious, healthy food, I drank all the water, I did everything I know how to do as a fitness professional with over a decade of experience, and I was *feeling* great, health wise. Yet, despite my obsessive efforts, I was somehow **gasp!** not an identical replica of my 27-year-old self, so in my head I felt horrible, and guilty, and frustrated, and sad, and angry. I felt all the feels. I felt it was somehow my sole purpose to a) keep my new tiny human alive, and b) get myself back into tip-top shape so it appeared as though I had never actually even been pregnant at all from an outside view. Those were my distorted priorities. That was the ridiculous goal I was hoping to achieve. The elusive comment from an outsider who would finally say "Wow! You don't even look like you *had* a baby!"

And of course, I agonized when it didn't happen the way I wanted it to. I shit-talked myself, over-and-over, and created a story that I was not good enough - because that's what my default mode dictated I should do. It's what I had done for years as I grew into a woman and tried my best to conform to what I thought was expected of my body and my appearance. It was easiest to go back to old patterns and tell myself I was a piece of crap because I was 40 pounds heavier than pre-baby and I was a shitty person because of it.

It has taken me a long time to process through those feelings, to smash the negative default-mode cycle, and to let go of all that previous judgement and criticism so I could move forward and get on with my life. It has taken a lot of practice and focused, determined mindset effort, but it can happen with the right energy in the right places. That's what I'm here to help you do.

I never did get the comment I was desperately longing for in all my interactions as a new mom navigating the world of motherhood and my obsessive get-my-pre-baby-bod-back cycle. Nobody ever gave me that ultimate compliment: *you don't even look like you had a baby*. I can't believe that's the number one priority I was striving for, but with the distorted perception I had about my body and how it should look to function in society, it was. And I never obtained what I was hoping for. But you know what?

IT'S OKAY.

It's okay. I realized it was okay and I adjusted my expectations. It didn't happen quite like that, quite that quick... but I did a lot of mind work. I read and listened to a lot of books. I continued to exercise, and I practiced different techniques for overcoming that judgement I was carrying around like a second child. I practiced. That's what self-love really is: a practice. It's ongoing. It's evolving. It's a journey. It has many paths. It has many seasons. If I can get across one thing to you in this book, it's that the road to confidence is paved with practice. And once you get into confidence-land, you circle back and continue the practice-paved-path over and over again, just like you train your muscles when you exercise. Confidence is like a muscle and requires dedicated practice. Practice requires focus and consistency. I want you to get to a point where you've made some drastic realizations, facilitated some much-needed change, and then continue to do what works for you to maintain that confidence for life.

What I slowly realized, and what I hope to convey

to you as we work on creating your very own arsenal of confidence-building techniques and strategies... that no *body* is ever "the same" forever. No woman is ever entirely the same from one period to the next. We all change. We all grow. We all develop. We change our minds, we work our bodies, we age, we take breaks, we relax, we make babies, we test our bodies with pregnancy (sometimes several times over), we get older naturally and gracefully and gain the wisdom and wrinkles that can only be acquired through a lifetime of laughter (and perplexing thoughts probably... because people be crazy), and we become different people. Why shouldn't our body be a bit different as we move through life?

I am a different person now than I was when I was 27. A better person. A stronger, wiser, more peaceful person. A mother to another person. You are too, right? *Phew.*

Once I came to this realization, I was able to let go. I quit being dragged by my pre-conceived notion of what I am "supposed to" look like after having a baby. I quit wondering if people noticed that I didn't "bounce back" as quickly as I "should" have. I quit assuming that people's opinion of me would somehow be better or worse based on my physical body. I stopped constantly assuming that the first thing someone would think when they saw me after some time had passed was that I was 20 pounds heavier than the last time they saw me.

(How obsessive is that?! Trust me, nobody cares enough to notice that much; to look that closely. To remember that you might "look different" than last time. Nobody.)

So this is you. This is your life. This is your body. It's the only you/life/body you have. You deserve love and acceptance from *your own self first*, and the truth is, the current circumstances are your reality, *right now*. So how are you going to treat *you*? Imma go ahead and help you re-position your perspective on that, mmkay? Great.

#MOMFIDENTAF

"This body was not created to be perfect, or fit into a pre-determined box, or look just like anybody else."

Chapter Two

A BRIEF HISTORY OF "MOMFIDENT AS F*CK"

What is "mom-fidence," anyway? What is the purpose of this term and what does it mean to have mom-confidence to the utmost degree? I'm so glad you asked! I think it's important to outline what you can expect to gain from this book before we get started. The way I see it, mom-confidence (herein "*momfidence*") includes a healthy and generally positive body image, learning the practice of embracing and accepting your postpartum body and self, and engaging regularly in self-love and self-care activities that make you feel damn good. It does have a lot to do with how you rock your mom-bod, with confidence. But it's also about feeling confident in your decision making skills, letting go of guilty feelings associated with your parenting choices or your constant craving for alone time, learning how to best support your life with encouraging connection circles, and editing the negative influences from your life so you can feel damn good more often. So, yes, having momfidence is partially about having body confidence, so we'll definitely touch on some practices for improving your overall body love strategy (...but don't worry, it doesn't include changing your body in some way before you can practice a high level of self-acceptance. We're here to work on the *now*, Sharon. Put your journal down). We're also going to discuss how different things we encounter in life influence and affect our *feelings* about our self and body-love; why you don't *feel* "good enough" in the first place; how you can actively notice what's affecting you so you can adjust your perspective; and how to let go of worrying what other people think so you can just do whatever you want to do, confidently. So you can let go of this idea that there's a specific way you're supposed to look, and just do the damn thang, with a kid on your arm, a smile on your face, and rocking the shit out of those high-waisted jeans.

So, "momfidence" is about living truly and authentically you, and feeling fucking good about it. It's about embracing your body **right now, as-is**, so that you can confidently evolve into whoever you want to be. It's about shutting down the mean-girl voice in your brain and re-writing the way you think about yourself, so you can feel damn good no matter what shape or size you are. It's about connecting to your body, being grateful for what you've got, and knowing that we're all in this together but we're all unique and incredible versions of this thing we call **human**. If you don't feel proud of the woman and mother you are today; if you struggle to strut your stuff on the beach because you're worried what someone might think about your rolls, cellulite or stretch marks; if you're constantly stressing about what you have compared to what other people have; and if your default mode is generally negative self-talk that drags you down instead of builds you up... then, girlfriend, you're ready to dig into this. I'm here for you. We're doing this together. My number one priority is getting you to think in a different way so you can make positive changes. And naturally, I'm confident *wink* my writing can provide that for you.

You may be curious about where the term, the brand, and the book *MOMFIDENT AS F*CK* came from. Well, here's the thing. I'm a Certified Fitness Professional and have worked in the fitness industry for nearly fifteen years. I worked in a high-level corporate management sector that developed and implemented group fitness programs for Canada's largest fitness facility for a better part of a decade. During that time, I worked one-on-one and privately with clients of all ages, shapes and sizes, and came to notice a huge gap in the industry that leaves people (mostly women) feeling unhappy and unfulfilled, no matter how successful they were in attaining their fitness goals. I saw countless women come into my classes and workshops, and they all felt the same way, even if they had just, for example, crushed an insurmountable weight loss goal. They still "felt fat", unworthy, not good enough, and set their sights on getting smaller and smaller in order to feel valuable. And then they would get smaller and smaller and still be unhappy. I saw women reach incredible weight-loss milestones, sometimes upwards of 100 pounds, and still see an overweight, and apparently undesirable woman looking back at her in the mirror, despite massive exterior changes. I also saw women show up, try for a few weeks, not see any immediate "visible" body progress, and quit. I saw women showing up for the sole purpose of changing their bodies, and then feeling frustrated when two cardio sessions didn't yield them any of those desired changes. I generally saw women connecting fitness and health to **only their exterior appearance**, and to nothing else at all.

This made me think. Hard. But I didn't do anything yet. I was only about 20 when I started vaguely noticing these things, and I had such a terrible body image myself and a very distorted perspective of what a healthy body looked like, so I couldn't quite connect the dots back then. I, too, still believed that the sole purpose of getting "healthy," changing your lifestyle, and working out regularly was primarily to change the shape of your body. I mean, duh, why else would you spend precious hours of your week torturing yourself in the gym?

In 2015, I became pregnant with my daughter, Presley, and though I did have a healthy and relatively uncomplicated pregnancy, I gained a lot of weight. Like, *a lot*. As someone who was already tall, broad, a size extra-large, overly body conscious, with messed up body ideals and a questionable relationship to fitness despite being a fitness instructor and manager for so many years... I didn't handle the weight gain well. It came on quickly and neared seventy pounds when I got to the end. I obsessed about it silently. I was insecure and sensitive to it. I was convinced everybody was talking about it behind my back. I heard my doctors cautiously questioning my eating habits and raising both eyebrows when they saw me step onto the scale at my monthly, then bi-weekly, then weekly appointments. There were weeks when I gained three pounds, and there were a few weeks where I gained nine or ten pounds. In a week! And that, coupled with the fact that I couldn't understand what I was doing to cause this type of weight gain, left me confused, frustrated, and ashamed that I was gaining so much weight. Shame. About gaining weight *during pregnancy*.

Everything was good, though, according to the

doctors. Technically. I was healthy and the baby was okay, but they were very concerned that I was tipping the scales at closer to 300 pounds in my third trimester. When I got pregnant, I was 200 pounds. That was also a lot of extra weight on my bones and joints for 76 long months. (Just kidding, I know it's only 9ish months. It felt like 76 though, especially on that ninth day overdue, *ya feel me!?*)

When I walked into the delivery room, I was swollen up so big the only way to describe how I felt was "Michelin Man." Okay, great, now you have an accurate visual.

I had spent most of my adult life chasing what I thought all women were supposed to be: "skinny." Working out with the sole intention of seeing body change. Going through very questionable eating habits and diets all in pursuit of getting as small as possible. This weight gain, albeit due to pregnancy, was not taken lightly. I felt terrible about myself on a daily basis, even though I knew I was carrying a healthy baby. It seemed at every moment, someone would mention to me that they'd only gained twenty pounds during their pregnancy. Someone told me she'd delivered and wound up weighing LESS THAN she did before getting pregnant that very same day. Someone else told me she'd gained twelve pounds total the entire nine months. *Twelve pounds!* HOW NICE FOR YOU, KAREN.

I knew that was not going to be me. As my newly acquired and self-proclaimed persona, the Michelin Man, I waddled into the delivery room and did what needed to be done. What followed was a very difficult postpartum experience and a lot of negative shit-thinking[4] that I didn't know how to deal with as I navigated becoming a new mom and also learning how the hell I was supposed to get rid of this new belly pooch. (See also: how the hell I was supposed to keep a new human alive, and also, who the hell I'm supposed to be now that I'm somebody's mom.)

I was already very hard on myself, as I think a lot of women are after years of subliminal messaging that we aren't good enough as-is and must immediately confirm to shape-shifting our bodies so that we look exactly like we just stepped out of a magazine in size zero Levis. Adding the extra weight gain, body changes, stretch marks, and idea I had in my head of what society expected of me in the months following my labour and

---

4 You read that right, I said shit-thinking. It's like shit-talk, but it's what happens inside your head. Nobody else notices, or has any idea you're doing it, but if you're not careful, it will spread and continually breed inside your head and all you'll think is shit-thoughts about yourself. Let's not, shall we? I'm going to get into the other parts - the stretch marks, the body image difficulties, how I started to transfer that energy, what I did to start thinking better things about myself, how I obsessed about fitness for a period and what it means to create a sustainable fit lifestyle, and even how I dealt with the leftover stretch marks I obtained during pregnancy... but for now, I just wanted you to have a brief insight to who I am and how I might be able to help you.

delivery (with the number one priority being, of course, "bounce back" to my pre-baby body as soon as I was out of the hospital), I knew I was in for a rough ride. I just didn't know that I had the power to change things inside, without changing things outside. I didn't know I could climate control my headspace and find a much more warm, accepting, and more loving temp to live in. I didn't know that self-acceptance was about more than just achieving the correct pants size and number on the scale. But I found all those things and more, and afterwards I felt a strong pull to start showing up with this message for other women who may have been feeling the same way as I once did.

Also in 2015, just before I had my daughter, I started a personal blog that evolved into a personal brand. What started as a diary of postpartum musings and sharing my daughter's milestones mostly for family, transformed into a brand about fitness, wellness, and health, based on my knowledge and career experience. The more I wrote, the more I understood what my audience wanted to hear, and it became clear that their favourite topics were less "how to burn 300 calories on the treadmill" and more how to obtain a positive body image, how to practice self-love, how to accept yourself, and how to embrace whatever skin you're in, right now. I did an overhaul in 2017 and shifted my brand dramatically from it's original title to "Body Momfidence." This was a risk, but luckily it landed well with my audience. After about a month of existing as "Body Momfidence" and starting "The Momfidence Podcast", I decided I wanted to talk about lots of different types of confidence, not just body confidence. I also decided I wanted to make it abundantly clear what my message was instead of tip-toeing around the topic. And one breezy afternoon in June of 2017, *MOMFIDENT AS F*CK* was born. A quick re-brand ensued and I began curating content to support the theme of confidence and helping women feel damn good about themselves, their bodies, and their lives, AS-IS. Confident as fuck, mom-style. (If you're wondering what the original title of my blog was, it was "Acorn & Coco." Yeah, not a very clear title for a health and wellness blog, right? "Acorn" and "Coco" are two nicknames I acquired by virtue of becoming an Aunt, and to this day I'm still called "Coco" by my nieces. They are both very important words to me, but not very clear for someone coming across my work.)

So, there you have it. That's where *MOMFIDENT AS F*CK* came from. I plan to continue evolving and, naturally, using my writing to help women just like you learn how to love themselves now, so they can live a brilliant, self-assured life that can only be describe as *MOMFIDENT AS F*CK*. Boom.

#MOMFIDENTAF

"Shit-thinking. It's like shit-talking, but it's what happens inside your head and nobody else knows you're doing it except you. Stop doing that 💩."

Change is not linear.

Before we like, officially dig into this thing, I want to give you a hard truth. The path to self-love, self-acceptance, embracing your body, and becoming hella confident in multiple areas of your life, is anything but linear. Much like the path to success, the path to living a life that you can only describe as *MOMFIDENT AS F*CK* is not something that you tackle from A to B to C and all the way to Z. Sorry, it just doesn't work that way. So while it'd be really nice and neat for me to package up this book into my "10 Steps to becoming Momfident As F*ck", it didn't happen for me that way and my guess is that it will not happen for you that way, either. There aren't logical steps. There's only assess, try, test, experiment, practice, and re-assess. If something works, you keep doing it. If it didn't work for you, no hard feelings. For that exact reason, you'll see this book flow from one truth to another, but there will not be a linear Step 1, Step 2, and Step 3 for you to follow with exact precision. That's on purpose, babe. There will be tips and suggestions for you to put into practice the things you learn, there will be real stories from my own "experiment" that may help you come to terms with something you're growing through; there will be a lot of sarcastic quips and conversational advice... but this is not a blueprint. You create your own blueprint.

I debated back and forth about creating specific

sections that deal with body, mind, and momlife, but I feel they just all bleed into one another anyway. Don't they? You could be feeling guilty about not going to the gym to improve your health because you can't find the time nor can you justify ditching your kids to "selfishly" focus on just you. Mind, body, mom life, mind, mom life, mind, in that order. It all works together. We have body image issues that often stem from adolescence, then we have kids, the body image issue grows, we lack self-care time because we have kids and busy lives, we don't take care of ourselves like we should, and then feel guilty when we actually do. We have 2,458,574 things on our to-do list at all times, so naturally we're stressed, overwhelmed, can't remember anything, are too tired to work-out and meal prep and the entire cycle begins again. I get it. Being a mom is hard, taking care of yourself (and literally everyone else) is hard, finding a good balance of the person you were before kids and the mom you want to be now... it's all fucking hard.

So in lieu of neatly packaged sections and chapters, you're going to see my own stories and realizations unfold much like they did on my own personal squiggly journey. And here's the other thing: my squiggly journey is actually not finished yet, either. I hope my recent footprints are able to help you navigate your way down your very own exclusive path, but know that the completion of a book does not signify the end of a journey.

Chapter Three
BODY LANGUAGE

When I was pregnant, suddenly it was like my growing body was suddenly fair game for unsolicited comments on a regular basis. The lady in line at the grocery store; someone in one of my group fitness classes; an aunt or uncle; a boss or colleague. It both bothered and shocked me, every time. I personally feel it's never okay to openly pass judgement on someone's appearance, *especially* a hormonal and probably overly sensitive pregnant woman. Right!? But this phenomenon isn't always reserved for pregnant woman. It may not be as common for someone to outwardly comment on the fact that you've gained weight, but people definitely congratulate you if you look like you've lost a few pounds. Don't they? "Have you lost weight?!" Somehow immediately becomes this kind of unsolicited yet coveted compliment, followed closely after the old "you look great!" Like, you couldn't possibly look great without the part where you appear to have lost weight. Humans are complicated and affected heavily by society and marketing; body language is tricky; and the "accomplishment" of being thin is on a ridiculous pedestal in our society. The next time you run into someone you haven't seen in a while, do me a favour and just say, "you look great!" Without any specific qualifier.

I'd like to say that women seem to be the most susceptible to getting comments about weight gain during pregnancy, and weight loss specifically as a compliment, but I think this affects everyone. I'm sure you have experienced this in some way, shape or form; maybe you've overheard a male friend or partner getting a compliment about building muscle like a badge of honour, or you've witnessed someone talk about a child who is "chunky" or alternatively, "a string bean." I wish we could set aside the comparison of bodies, the glorification of "skinny," and just allow people to exist in their shape no matter what it looks like against anyone else. But, unfortunately, this is something we all deal with on a regular basis, and it deserves some attention, especially as it pertains to how the hell you're supposed to manage it when it happens.

Outside of the too-many-to-count comments I

received while I was pregnant, I've encountered one person in my entire life that had the balls enough to casually spit out his honest unfiltered observation that it looked like I'd "put on a few, eh?" since the last time I saw him. Well, I had. I think, anyway - I don't weigh myself anymore. At the time, I was too fragile and insecure to say anything back. I didn't have the confidence to counter with a spicy rebuttal (and it was also embarrassing, uncomfortable, and hurtful, which generally causes me to flight versus fight), so I just walked away from the situation to avoid answering. I really, *really* wish I had said something, though, and I hope you'll learn from my avoidance and be sharp and witty if someone dares to make a comment about how your external appearance has changed over time. Here's what I wish I'd said. I feel pretty proud of it, so go ahead and steal it if you like. AHEM: "Well, yeah, dickwad (JK, but seriously), I probably have, thanks for noticing. What I've really gained though is a non-judgemental perspective about my own body that isn't weight-focused, and knowledge of how to live at peace with it, no matter what size it is. Good thing, too, because otherwise I'd really have taken personal offence to your comment and probably would be crying in the bathroom right now and avoiding eating anything for the next two weeks. Just so you know, that's what comments about size can do to vulnerable women. Ass."

Let's talk a little more about why other people's comments about body shape affect us on such a grand scale. If someone, *anyone* says something like this to you, you have a choice for how you handle it. You can walk away, like I did, and allow it to seep into your soul and self-worth, or you can speak up and be just as straightforward as this person is being with you. At the end of the day, a comment about weight fluctuation *shouldn't* affect us; we *shouldn't* take personal offence to it; we shouldn't get emotional and upset, but the truth is we've been conditioned our entire female lives that gaining weight = bad, and losing weight = good. The only time in my life I've ever received compliments on my physical appearance was when I was at my lowest weight due to an extremely unhealthy lifestyle I strictly adhered to in order to fit that body ideal I talked about earlier. I was fitting it, *finally*, but my behaviours were obsessive and restrictive and exceptionally unhealthy. Everyone was praising me for my body shape and perpetuating that long-held belief that small was better than big. Their comments rewarded me for being hella restrictive, obsessing over anything that went into my mouth, training at the gym for 2-3 hours at a time, sometimes more than once a day, spending hours picking myself apart in the mirror with disgust, and emulating extremely disordered eating habits. Great. It was like I'd reached the apparent ultimate goal, but in order to do so, I had to do terrible things to my body, because my body is not meant to be a size four. And then someone would come along and say "Wow, Court, you look amazing!" and it was more fuel for powering my ridiculous, obsessive, restrictive lifestyle habits.

We will never be able to control what other people think, say, or do, so I don't want you to spend your time worrying about it. In the off chance that someone *does* notice your body has changed in some way, and openly shares their observation with you... *so what?* I know it can hurt, but their acknowledgement, though it may actually be true, is so tiny on the list of "fucks you should give" and I promise you, it does not deserve your energy or attention. Plus, why would you want to hang around with someone like that, if they're outrageously stupid enough to TELL someone, a woman at that, that she appears to have gained weight, considering the societally-generated negative connotation of gaining weight? *Believe me, Brenda, I'm aware of my body shape and if anyone notices a change, it's me. I don't need you to announce it to me. Thanks, though.* When it comes to the topic of "weight gain" vs "weight loss" the regularly perpetuated consensus seems to be that people favour weight loss and use it as a compliment when meeting after some time, so we have a lot of work to do in this area. Any comment to the contrary seems like it's just meant for shade-throwing. That's not a person I care to have in my corner.

For the most part, though, you will not be able to tell what anybody else is thinking and so, it's high time we start letting that shit go. The definition of insanity might need a minor edit: "Doing the same thing over and over, and expecting different results... and/or trying to assume you could possibly know the thoughts of another human being other than yourself." - Edited, 2019. I am so much more than just what I look like. You are so much more than just what you look like.

You feel me, girl?

I thought so.

Alright, so pregnancy and the impending changes it likely caused to your body, weight, and skin was definitely hard, but then this thing called "postpartum" comes along and I think you'll agree that this is when the real shit show begins. Not only are you responsible for taking care of another person, but you're supposed to figure out how to navigate your day-to-day with someone attached to you at the ~~hip~~ boob. Of course, there's the whole figuring-out-what-babies-need thing, but there's also: trying to figure out if you should continue to wear maternity clothes or struggle to squeeze back into your own oversized sweatpants; trying to take a shit for the first time after your vagina has been ripped apart; remembering to feed yourself; wanting to scroll the gram, and tidy the pile of baby clothes on the kitchen table simultaneously; somehow entertain multiple guests at a time, even though you know you are supposed to "sleep when the baby sleeps"; figuring out how to breastfeed (if you choose and are able to) approximately sixty-seven hours a day through raw, bleeding, painful nips; leaving your keys in the fridge and your coffee in the shower and not finding either until days later; and navigating it all through the added effect of a) baby blues, b) raging hormones, c) postpartum anxiety, d) postpartum depression, or e) any combination of the above.

So while "joining the mother-hood" and pushing a baby out your vag is definitely hard, it wasn't the most difficult part, for me. Nope. Because, now, I actually have to figure out how to handle this motherhood thing, and with that comes a lot of difficult shit (and not just that actual first shit, which is terrifying in and of itself.) Not only are we finding ourselves as a mothers and perhaps as a different-ish partner than we were pre-baby, we also have to learn what the hell to do with this new, changed body. That's a lot of shit to handle.

I, like you, I assume, was just as judgemental and critical on myself in the months following my labour and delivery as I had been on my body for most of my adult life. Except now, there was even more change to deal with. I didn't know what to do, I only knew I felt like shit about myself constantly. I couldn't look at myself when I stepped out of the shower. I felt like a stranger in my own body. I didn't know how to dress myself, and when I had to, I was irrationally emotional about it. None of my clothes fit. I could barely see my own vagina over my belly that still looked six months pregnant, even weeks after I came home from the hospital. I couldn't bear to look at my newly acquired stretch marks and I was trying to figure out how to handle these new milk-filled (and sometimes painful) boobs. I was dealing with some real identity issues, both questioning who I was as a new mom, and who I physically showed up as in the world. I constantly worried what other people thought of me and stressed over the fact that I literally was living in a different body than they'd likely seen me in before.

I pushed myself to the gym as soon as I could and agonized over the painfully slow progress I was making. Achieving a body that looked just like the one I had before conceiving was at the top of my to-do list. I didn't want my husband to take pictures of me with my new baby, and I almost missed the opportunity to get into a photo with Presley at our newborn session. If it weren't for my amazing photographer gently encouraging me to jump in there, I wouldn't have a single photo that included me from that entire session. This was not a way to live. It was not a way that I wanted to show up for my daughter. It was not the example I wanted to set for her or anyone else. Something had to change, and since my body wasn't doing what I wanted it to, as fast as I expected it to, I realized it was time to create some change elsewhere. I couldn't continue down this path of self-loathing, negative self-talk, and ultimately self-hatred, just because my body had retained a few pounds. It was a journey that extended for nearly four years, but as I started to gain clarity about my self-worth and value outside my appearance, I began to build my confidence from the inside out. I learned a few things along the way that changed the game for me, and that's what I'm about to share with you throughout the rest of this book.

#MOMFIDENTAF

"You will never be able to tell what anybody else is thinking and so, it's high time you start letting that shit go. Now. Like, right nnnnow."

Chapter Four

EFFECTIVE HANDLING OF CHANGING BODS

Now, again, the whole motherhood thing should not have thrown me for a loop, considering I knew this was coming for about, oh, *nine months exactly*, and, as most women do, I started getting pretty aware of my bod changing around the six months mark, and that's when I started getting ~~a bit~~ obsessively panicky about the fact that I might acquire some stretch marks on my, up until this point, basically unmarked twenty-seven-year-old body. I used all the creams. I drank all the water. I slathered bio-oil on there like bio-oil doesn't cost like $40 a bottle. (Seriously, why is bio-oil that expensive?) I was doing everything I was "supposed to" do, to avoid the thing that everybody spends too much precious time worrying about: stretch marks. Dear Lord, don't let me get any stretch marks, PLEASE. I remember thinking I had strutted smoothly into my third trimester without nary a stretch mark to my name, and I felt strangely "proud" of myself, as if it's any kind of accomplishment to avoid the inevitable. Stretch marks, my dear friends, are more about genetics than they are about how much water you drink, how much cocoa butter and bio-oil you can slather on yourself, and whether your bump is long and tall or short and wide. Girl, preach.

Anyway, one day when I was probably about 32 weeks pregnant, something weird was happening "down below" and I thought I should probably take a look down there to see what was going on. So, after an evening shower, while sitting on the edge of my bed in just a towel, I took a hand mirror down there to check it out.

Everything was fine down there (you know, in case you were wondering...) but what I wound up seeing, to my surprise, with great horror and without actually meaning to see, was that pretty much every square inch of skin underneath my belly button was covered with stretch marks. I hadn't been able to see that part of my stomach for many months, and so because I couldn't see under there I thought I'd escaped pregnancy stretch-mark free, especially since I had made it so far along. I felt like I had some kind of "stretch-mark-avoidance" success, like that was one of the main priorities in growing a baby. Like I'd somehow "won" the stretch-mark-free lottery and someone was going to walk in with a trophy and award me for achieving such elusive standards. BUT NO. Darn. Tough luck.

What happened next, you ask? I lost my shit. I started freaking out. I started crying profusely (which could also have been due to hormones but, still), and then my husband came in and panicked like something had gone wrong.

When I told him, through gasp-y ugly-cry breaths and tear-streaked cheeks: "I have 8 billion stretch marrrrrrrrks!!!" He laughed.

THAT MOTHER FUCKER *LAUGHED!*

He couldn't understand why I was so upset. He literally had not a single clue why having stretch marks would be *any* cause for concern, let alone the dramatic waterworks. He was like, "what did you expect? You're pregnant!"

I was of course then immediately mad at him for being insensitive and "acting like an asshole", and sulked in my bed for the rest of the night, sporadically re-living the moment and then having bouts of panick-y PTSD sob sessions as I thought about it over and over again.

When I think about this episode now, I realize I was overreacting, of course, but I can certainly understand how someone suddenly coming to the realization that they have a tummy full of "dreaded" stretch marks could be upsetting. And back then, I had a much more negative self-image than I do today, and that's because I didn't practice any of the techniques I share about today.

Appearance was everything to me back then. I was constantly on a quest to act and react based on what I thought it would do for my outward appearance *only*. I dyed my hair blonde because I thought blondes were more attractive. I was an extreme dieter and ate things with the purpose of hoping I'd lose weight, or look a certain way, and not for the true purpose of eating: to fuel my body. I exercised only to lose weight, never for any other reason. I would quit whatever program or routine I was on briefly when I noticed the scale stopped moving, and lose all motivation to keep going because it wasn't providing me the end goal I was expecting. I would whiten my teeth way too often, even though my teeth are naturally pre-disposed to being white (thanks, Dad!) I would stare at myself in the mirror and take mental images of when I "sucked it in" vs. "let it hang out" and would obviously prefer the former image. I would shop for clothes and buy smaller sizes, so that I could "diet" my way into them. I was obsessed with my eyebrows, with having my nails done always, my legs shaved, my skin tanned to a glow-y sun-kissed colour, even in February.

So, of course, when I noticed that the stretch mark fairy had blessed me with more of them than I could count, I took it personally. I reacted as if life, as I knew it, was over.

Which is *ridiculous*. But understandable.

Our society is a culture of expectation. Expectation that women have certain roles, expectation that we achieve certain things, expectation that we make specific decisions. And, something that we typically find the hardest to manage personally: expectation that real women look like women in magazines, on television, and on social media. It's really hard for us, subconsciously, to process the fact that every image we see in the media is a curated, photoshopped, nipped, tucked, filtered, and edited version of reality. Even if you don't think you're affected by it, over time, it eats away at you. You think there's something wrong with your cellulite because whether you notice it or not, not a single image you see includes cellulite. You think there's something wrong with your teeth because the only examples of teeth you see are perfect, white, and straight. You think there's something wrong with your stretch marks because everything you see is perfectly flawless, smooth, and even-toned. You think there's something wrong with your freckles, your moles, your birth mark, your uneven skin tone, or your bumpy bikini line, because the examples of bodies you're exposed to do not have any imperfections or flaws. Ever.

I'd like to mention that if there's something about

yourself that bothers you so much that you want to improve it, by all means, go for it. If you have wanted braces your whole life, and you have the means to afford it, then hot damn, get braces! Imperfection is beauty and we're all uniquely beautiful. We are just exposed so rarely to the beautiful realities of normal human traits, that we think "normal bodies" and "beautiful people" are only what we see in the magazines and on TV, and, honey - it's all an illusion. The moment you can begin to detach your self-worth from the external image of yourself, is the moment you can begin to curate a more natural, positive, and healthy self-image. Don't let straight teeth be what you're waiting for as the missing piece that will allow you to somehow *finally* become confident. Don't let losing 30 pounds be the "thing" that, when accomplished, will *finally* make you feel good about yourself. I want you to work on feeling good about yourself. Right. Fucking. Now. That means pounds, rolls, stretch marks, freckles, teeth, rogue eyebrows, cellulite, discolouration, razor burn, ingrown hairs, acne, unkempt nails and facial hair, roots and whatever hair colour you were born with. I know, I know. It's easier said than done. But it is do-able.

There's another thing that plagued me, even up until as recently as a year ago. After having my daughter, I was left with a belly "pooch" that many moms get after childbirth. At first, I was so frustrated with it and irritated that no matter how much I worked out and ate "properly", it didn't go away. I slaved for hours at the gym. For the last three months of my maternity leave, I packed up my baby and spent two full hours at the gym every single day of the week. I didn't feel successful until I had done an hour of specific muscle group weight training, and then at least 60 minutes of hard cardio, steady-state running, intervals, hill sprints, and the like. I felt like a fraud for being a fitness professional who didn't "bounce-back" immediately following the birth of my child. I felt like a failure for having a 9-month-old and still not being back to my pre-pregnancy weight or fitting fully into my pre-pregnancy clothes. Getting "back" was my top priority, above all else.

After all those obsessive gym sessions for three months straight, first and foremost, I got back to my exact pre-pregnancy weight (which was 200 pounds, if you'll recall.) But you know what? The belly pooch didn't really go away, and I agonized over it. I beat myself up about it. Hard. I judged and criticized and shit-thought myself every chance I got. If you'd looked at me from the outside (as I can do now, having perspective) you'd have thought I was crazy to agonize over something so miniscule. I had some of the elusive 'definition' the fitness world raves about (ahem, *some* being the operative word here, my body is not really programmed for abs) but there was still a bit of extra skin and body fat that pooched out over my underwear. Another person wouldn't have even noticed it. I, on the other hand, drained all my energy worrying about how it looked. And do you know what else? When I went back to my normal routine and re-joined the work force, I couldn't keep up with this ridiculous workout plan I had been abiding by, because it was incredibly outrageous and unrealistic for life balance. I didn't have 2 hours in my day, every single day, seven days a week, to spend on fitness anymore. It wasn't a sustainable schedule for me to maintain, so I put about 15 pounds back on in the first few months back to work. I already had issues with one teeny, tiny, minuscule body trait that I'd determined was a "flaw," and then I dared to gain *more* weight. And again, I beat myself up about it. Hard.

Here's the thing that we don't talk about enough, and especially we don't heave about enough at the pursuit of the gym-joining process. You have a very distinct set of genetics. Your body has a specific weight range that it will naturally fall into, once you get into the rhythm of fuelling your body well and moving it regularly. But if you try to go outside (AKA, super far below) the natural weight range you're meant for, it will be extremely difficult to maintain, and will likely result in a short term success that will be difficult to keep up with forever. And so begins the Yo-Yo cycle. The fitness industry also does not talk about how in order to be fit and healthy, it isn't a prerequisite to have the same body as anybody else, to have visible abs or any other visible muscles, or to be a certain size or weight. All bodies can be healthy, and they'll all be healthy in their own way. Your healthy lifestyle + your genetics lottery = your own, very unique fit body. Maybe it includes a belly pooch. Maybe it's 30% body fat. Maybe it's a size four. Maybe it's a size sixteen. It will never, ever, look exactly like anybody else's fit body.

So, yeah, I got down to a very low weight for my body. Mission accomplished, as it were. Mind you, I didn't feel good about myself at *all* despite all my hard work. And then, it was even harder to handle when I gained 15 pounds. Talk about a mental struggle bus. Because I had decided that I was only worthy, valuable, and capable of self-acceptance when I was paired with a certain, very specific weight, I did not think I was good enough when I gained some. My expectation was that I worked out, I ate well, and I should lose weight. A certain amount of weight, to be exact. So now is the time where I tell you that small does not equal happy. Weight loss does not equal fulfillment. All your problems do not magically go away if you get rid of every imperfection you've ever had. If you don't work on the shit that goes on inside your brain, no amount of external change will adjust how you feel about yourself. I can promise you that.

#MOMFIDENTAF

"If you don't work on the shit that goes on inside your brain, no amount of external change will adjust how you feel about yourself."

Chapter Five
ACCEPTING YOUR NOW

Let me ask you something. If you stood in the mirror, right this second, completely naked, and looked at your current body (pre-, post-, or regardless of pregnancy at all), would it make you *happy*? Would it, as Marie Kondo might say, "spark joy?" Would you feel *grateful* to have experienced the miracle of pregnancy and childbirth? Would you feel proud of the vessel that carries your incredible mind, thoughts, and strength? Would you be able to look at yourself and claim your profound love for your body? Would you be able to look at yourself without picking your body apart and without judgement, criticism, and negativity? Would "happy", "grateful", "proud" and "love" be words you'd use to describe your body *right this very moment?*

If I said that you would be stuck forever with the body that you have **right now**, as you're reading this, would you be okay with it? I put this question out on one of my early podcast episodes, and the response to this particular question drew an overwhelming amount of discussion. Many women shared that they felt it was the "wake up call" they needed to finally "get in gear" and start making the right decisions and choices that would get them closer to a body they could truly love and appreciate.

That isn't the purpose of this question. At all.

What I was trying to get my listeners to think about was the fact that they are capable of love and acceptance *even if* they don't yet have the aesthetic they long for. *Even if* they don't have a "perfect" body. *Even if* they are 10, 20, 50 pounds heavier than they'd ideally prefer to be.

The thing is, it's okay to desire change for your body. It is! There has been a lot of misconception in the popularization of the body positivity movement that makes it seem as though loving your current body and size is about accepting it as-is and then... what? You just give up? You never desire change, or want to grow, or be a better person, or have interest in evolving yourself ever again? You are never allowed to want to make some changes to your life that will impact you for the better? You don't need to think about how you feed your body and if you move it regularly?

I want you to always begin with love. To start with love, as the foundation. I want you to learn how to love, accept, and embrace your body and yourself as-is, so that if and when you want to make changes, you approach them from a place of love, not loathing. This is something I call "abundance" versus "lack" health mindset. It's so important to love the skin you're in NOW, instead of waiting to feel love for it once it's changed for you. Change should not precede acceptance.

I've operated from a place of "lack" for as long as I can remember. Lack is when you don't have something that you want. Here are a few examples. You could think that you can't start that Network Marketing business because there isn't enough to go around, so why should you bother to start? That's assuming there aren't enough customers or people to go around, and is a poor mentality to walk around with. That's a lack opportunity mindset.

You could have been taught that "money doesn't grow on trees" as a kid, if your parents were strapped for cash and never had as much of the green stuff as they wanted. You may have grown up thinking money is hard to obtain, difficult to achieve, and therefore, there isn't a lot of it for the taking. That's assuming there isn't enough money for you. That's a lack money mindset.

And, similarly, there's a lack mindset as it pertains to your body. If you have a body that you don't like, and you'd prefer a different one - that's wanting something you don't currently have. That's "lack" mentality. When we approach change, like wanting to lose weight for example, from a lack mentality, we're chasing after something we want that we don't already have. We lack it. We want it. And we're obsessing over getting it. This equation of lack + want adds up to great disappointment in general. We don't have the body we want, so that drives us to make some changes in order to acquire it. The problem is, were operating under the pretence that we don't currently like the body we have. Right? We want a different one, badly, because we're unhappy with the one we have. We're desperate to change it so that everything magically gets better in our lives. We want to change it so that we can then (and only then) accept it. NEWSFLASH: Everything does not magically get better just because you change your external body. *Raises hand* Speaking from experience, here.

Contrast the lack mentality with an abundance perspective. When you live in abundance, you believe that you have everything you need, you trust that things and opportunities and money and desires are coming to you, you work hard but you don't stress or compare or worry that you won't get what you need. You believe it will come. So, if we can set our sights on an abundance health mindset, we start thinking that maybe, we already have everything we need. Maybe, our bodies are just fine as they are. Maybe, we don't need to stress about obtaining a version of fit that doesn't work for us or that's ridiculously difficult to obtain. Maybe, we are good, right now, as-is. And if we want to make fitness a priority and set a weight loss goal, so be it. But we're approaching it from a place of abundance, of happiness, of acceptance and of love, not a place of lack and hate. Not a place of judgement. Not a place of criticism. Remember, I'm not saying you can't or shouldn't desire a change in your body. You can want whatever you want. I am, however, asking you to consider how you approach making a change, and that you spend some time committing to the *love* part of the equation, first. Because, you can't hate yourself into loving yourself. Can you? I mean, I think if you could, nobody would need this book and you wouldn't be reading this right now.

So the first thing we need to do is *always* start with love. Begin with love. Commence par l'amour. When I teach on this topic, I use a concept called "Embrace and Evolve". The first step is to embrace, and that's typically the work we do to begin loving ourselves fully, working on our mindset, learning how to be less judgemental, less critical, less hard on ourselves, and getting rid of the negative self-talk and shit-thinking that we do on a regular basis. All of this comes in the first part, the "embrace" part. It's the groundwork, the foundation to acceptance and feeling good in our own skin.

The second part is about the change. It's the part where we may want to grow as a person. We may want to develop, or build our knowledge. Or, maybe we do want to change our bodies in some way. But with all the embracing we've done first, all the groundwork we've laid, we aren't approaching our desired "evolution" from a place of lack or hate or shame. We're now approaching it from a place of love instead.

Embrace can come before evolve, and embrace and evolve can co-exist, but evolve never comes before embrace. Trying to "make yourself better" in some way, when you are operating at a place of lack, negativity, disgust, judgement, or unhappiness about yourself, is more hindrance than help. It perpetuates the idea that you are not worthy or good enough *until* you make the change you're trying to make during your "evolution". That's ass-backwards from what I'm trying to suggest to you. Embrace first. Or even, embrace while you evolve. But don't try to evolve before you embrace. Please.

Lack mindset says, "I hate my body, and I want it to look different. I need it to look different so that I can un-hate myself. I want it to look like something I don't currently have." So, we often do unhealthy things in the pursuit of acquiring that external change, because we're unhappy with the way we are and we think obtaining that thing that we lack will fix it. We try to hate our bodies into the version we'd prefer instead.

All we do is fixate on how much we believe we'll be happier with ourselves when we shift our body into looking a different way. But: *You. Can't. Hate. Yourself. Into. Loving. Yourself...* (one more time for the mamas in the back!) and no amount of body change is going to change the way you feel, speak, and think about yourself. Trust me. I've been a size 6 and a size 16, and there was actually far more criticism, hate, and unhappiness at the smaller size. On the other hand, abundance mindset says, "I already have everything I need. My body is perfect, strong, and good just the way it is. I am going to make some healthy changes that will impact my overall health, and if the external changes because of it, that's great! But I'm happy with who I am. I respect and appreciate who I am, right now. External changes may come and go, and I'll continue to be happy with myself either way." And we operate with a much healthier outlook, we make slow progress, and we view our healthy lifestyle as a journey, not a destination. Because we believe we already have everything we need, and trust that if we work towards our goals, we'll achieve them.

Your "healthy journey" will look different than mine and your mom's and your best friend's. We'll talk more on the importance of health for your mind and your body later, but let's hang here for a minute in the land of building a "healthy mindset." If there's one thing you take away from this section, let it be this: **your mind will believe whatever you tell it.** So if you internally shit-think yourself 'round the clock, is it any real surprise that you have the outlook on yourself that you do? Is it shocking that you regularly call yourself negative things, think you aren't good enough, call yourself fat or ugly or stupid without a second thought, and don't feel good about yourself? Is it surprising that you look at specific areas of your body and instead of practicing acceptance, you practice judgement and hate? If you changed the thoughts inside your head, your brain would believe those things too, but unfortunately most of our default-mode thinking is about how we don't measure up in some way.

As you approach the next section, I want you to keep this idea stored somewhere in your head... preferably somewhere that's easily accessible and not, like, somewhere equivalent to storage in the "cloud." Nobody knows where things in the cloud go. *Your mind will believe whatever you tell it.* It's time to start observing the things you're telling yourself, and find out if they're helpful or hurtful. That's a great place to start.

#MOMFIDENTAF

"It's so important to love the skin you're in NOW, instead of waiting to feel love for it once it's changed for you. Change should not precede acceptance."

Chapter Six

GETTING CONFIDENT (AF)

So, here's the thing. Contrary to popular belief, confidence is not reserved for people who only have "perfect bodies". There really isn't such thing as a "perfect" body anyway, but the quest for the perfect body is what drives many to an extremely unhealthy relationship with themselves, and their confidence. Confidence is available to everybody. Having what Western society has dictated as a "good-looking" appearance does not equal confidence, and you are 1000% capable of building and maintaining confidence even if you don't fit the mold of that "perfect" aesthetic. I know of many strong, powerful, confident women who do not have perfect bodies or a perfect appearance, and are completely happy and content with themselves, because they've come to love and accept their uniqueness and worry less about how they stack up to anyone else. It's honestly more of an attitude than anything else, babe. Seriously! On the flip side, I've also known incredibly insecure women who are absolutely drop dead gorgeous with the elusive and socially acceptable "thin" frame who cannot seem to see their own value or worth, despite having what everybody on the outside looking in assumes is a "perfect" life because of their natural beauty and (maybe) great genetics. Perfection does not equal confidence. Confidence is like a muscle that must be trained regularly, just like any other muscle in your body, and it's available for you, too.

Let's clear up another misconception about confidence, ASAP. Confidence is not exclusively paired with being "outgoing." Having an outgoing personality is not a byproduct of confidence, and an outgoing person is not necessarily confident. People often confuse these two and assume that when someone is outgoing, friendly, easy to talk to, loud, and enjoys being at the centre of all the attention, they are automatically the most confident person in the room. Not true. Just as a shy quiet person chilling in the corner of the party is not necessary the most insecure and "unconfident" person, either. You don't need the outgoing personality trait in order to show up feeling great in your own skin and letting that radiate from you 24/7. It also isn't a prerequisite to outwardly announce (loudly, at that) your newfound state of self-acceptance, regardless of whether you're an outgoing gal or a strong silent type. Nobody expects a confident person to walk into a room and say "Hi, everybody! Look at me! Look how confident I am!" In fact, I would argue that there are some of you who have an inherent outgoing personality and have a severe lack of confidence, and perhaps you even use being loud and funny and the centre of attention as a defence mechanism. Perhaps you feel embarrassed or ashamed by any insecurities you have developed, so it's easier to be known as the "funny one" instead of dealing with the real shit. I'm not pointing any fingers, bro, just stating some hard facts.

Whether you enjoy being at the centre of it all (more extroverted), or prefer to sit quietly and socialize less (introverted), "quiet confidence" is something we can all work on building. It doesn't scream from the rooftops; it whispers (confidently) from the baseline, more or less.

"Arrogance requires advertising. Confidence speaks for itself."

—Dr. Farrah Gray

For your reference, I've compiled a list of things you absolutely do NOT need, in order to be a confident, self-assured woman:

- to have a perfect body
- to be thin

- to be the most attractive person in the room
- to be the "outgoing" or extroverted type
- to loudly announce how you feel about yourself to anyone

Confidence in itself contributes to the appeal of somebody, regardless of what they look like. Have you ever been strangely attracted to someone even though you didn't initially think, based only on their looks alone, that they would be someone you'd be interested in? Regardless of your sexual preference, have you ever been oddly attracted to someone who you wouldn't normally find desirable, regardless of gender, and you weren't really sure why or how? There's a very good chance that was confidence at play. There's something so attractive about confidence.

Pardon me, I'd guess I should clarify, it was probably *quiet* confidence. There's a difference between loud and quiet confidence, isn't there? Loud confidence is more like cockiness, ego, and conceit; quiet confidence is humble, kind, and non-braggy. It could have literally been ONLY because of the person's confidence. Confidence is the fucking sexiest thing a person can wear. Period.

Remember a few chapters ago when I asked you if you could love and accept your body, exactly as-is, *right now*? It was not to make you re-consider your life choices and start getting up at 5am to do cardio every day in order to drop 15 pounds right-quick so you'd *fiiiinally* feel good about yourself.

No, girl, NO!

(I mean… if that's what you want to do with your precious 5am time, more power to you. But that's not what I was suggesting.)

My point was that confidence needs to be born and bred from the *inside* out, not the other way around. You need to start being **okay with yourself** no matter what size or shape you are; no matter how many scars; no matter how many stretch marks; no matter what number is on the scale and no matter what your clothes look like. It might start out as quietly tolerating yourself, and may not be a full-blown self-obsession right out of the gate. But I want you to understand that you absolutely cannot wait for your body to be "perfect" before you consider how you could *possibly* be confident with yourself the way you are in this moment. You'll be waiting forever, trust me. Perfection does not equal confidence; size does not guarantee confidence; and all the things you're waiting to go after until you're "skinnier," all the things you want but think you don't deserve in your current body, all the prior thought patterns that have said, "If I can just lose this weight then I'll be able to _____," or that everything will be fixed or solved in your life when you reach that "goal weight"… none of that is true. I'm telling you from experience, it is absolutely, fully, completely, *untrue*. Nothing gets better just because you change your body or your appearance. But things can get *far* better if you change your mindset.

Now hear me out with yet another disclaimer-type paragraph, okay? This is important. The dichotomy between feeling good and looking good is one worth exploring, and I don't intend to skip over the fact that yes, you *can* affect and even increase positive feelings about yourself by making lifestyle changes that may impact your weight. Sure. I'm not trying to suggest that you can't or shouldn't make necessary or desired changes to yourself or your body. I would also never suggest that you turn a blind eye to unhealthy behaviours in the pursuit of just loving your body as-is. As we discussed earlier, planning to evolve in some way, including evolving your body if you wish, is totally A-OK in my books, as long as you approach it from a place of love. If you are truly unhappy with your vessel, the good news is that you DO have the ability to change it. YOU DO! Isn't that amazing?! If losing weight, or fitting into a sexy dress 2 sizes down from what you currently wear, or if losing five pounds so you can feel better in your bathing suit is important to you and would truly fulfill you, then you should ABSOLUTELY go for it! But external change cannot be your sole driver. It just can't be.

I hope I'm not confusing you. The bottom line is

that moving your body and eating nutritious foods is majorly important to your health. Super important. Like, vital. Make no mistake about that. I will always promote fitness, and I believe that every *body* needs movement on a regular basis. (And my personal beliefs aside, any health professional would tell you that too. I don't care if you're walking every day or hitting the gym 4x/week; weight training, swimming, or taking Zumba classes. It's very important to incorporate movement in your routine.) I've been a fitness instructor for nearly fifteen years and I still coach fitness online. However, we cannot place our hopes and dreams on achieving the perfect body. We cannot fall victim to fitness marketing that tells us we MUST lose 20 pounds in order to be attractive and accepted. Weight loss should not be for aesthetic reasons, but unfortunately that's what we've been told our whole lives.

Normal alert: Your weight is going to fluctuate at different periods of your life, for different reasons. It's human and totally normal to have some weight fluctuations through different life-stages, experiences, circumstances, and seasons. If you've built up your confidence from the inside out, you will be able to be happy with yourself no matter what size, and radiate that confident energy throughout the room like nobody's business, every time. People will notice it. People will notice you. There's nothing more beautiful than a confident soul.

#MOMFIDENTAF

"Confidence needs to be born and bred from the inside out, not the other way around."

Chapter Seven

MINDSET SHIFTS. THEY'RE LIKE, SO FETCH.

I want you to **change your mind** about your**self**.

Like, right now.

No, I'm not kidding. Do it!

Okay, okay, I know it isn't like turning on a light switch. But it begins with the simple decision to change. Right now, at this very moment, you are officially no longer available for thinking negative shit about your beautiful, healthy, strong, powerful, sexy self, which includes your body. Awareness breeds change, so we begin with the awareness that you already have all the power you need to change your mind about yourself and your body, and it's totally, fully, and completely, up to **YOU**.

Not there yet? Stick with me, okurrr?

Your mindset is quite possibly the most powerful and malleable tool you have in the toolbox of life. At any given moment, you can decide to change it. Without notice, without explanation. You can change it, whenever you want. So as you travel along your personalized path to becoming the most ~~confident mom~~ momfident person you can be, I want you to remember this: only **you** have the power to change your mind.

(Well, you and sometimes a really convincing bottle of wine. But, mostly, just you.)

You can change your mind whenever you damn well feel like it. I know, it's a groundbreaking revelation, but sometimes it just takes another person to say something out loud, and you see things in a different way. And to clarify, I don't mean "change your mind" like, change your opinion on something. I don't mean, you were planning to go to the gym today but you "changed your mind" and stayed at home instead. I mean *really* change it. Change how it operates. Change its default mode. Change your thought process. Change your attitude. Change your perspective, your mood, your entire mindset. Your thoughts can (and do) manifest into reality. Where do you want to spend your precious mind-money?

Have you ever thought so hard about something that you *didn't* want to happen, and then it wound up happening anyway? The last time this happened to me, it was thinking I didn't want to get sick. My daughter was sick, my husband was sick, everybody around me seemed to be sick, and all I could think of was "don't get sick, don't get sick, don't get sick."

You know what happened? SHOCKER! I got sick. For fuck sakes. (I mean, that wasn't just "manifestation," it was probably science too. Spreading germs and stuff. Fiiine.)

Another time, I was driving somewhere and noticed I was speeding. Oopsie. Going quite a few clicks over the old speed limit, in fact. I slowed down a little, thinking that I might see a cop, because I'm being a bad girl and speeding. Then I forgot and resumed my speed. I kept thinking, "I don't want to see a cop, I don't want to see a cop, I don't want to see a cop…"

Guess what? I saw a cop. He pulled me over. I got a ticket.

DAMMIT.

This is like, the science of the universe though. For real. When you spend a lot of your time focusing hard on something, it can actually happen. I'm not exaggerating, it's a real thing. It's sort of like backwards-manifestation, except often we waste our precious time and energy thinking about the things we *don't* want to happen. Ideally, if you're going to manifest anything, it should probably be something you *do* want to happen. Your brain is naturally triggerd by hearing the thing you don't want over and over on repeat.

Manifestation:

[noun man·i·fes·ta·tion \ ˌma-nə-fə-ˈstā shən , -ˌfe-ˈstā- \ ]
1 a : the act, process, or an instance of manifesting; demanded some manifestation of repentance[5]

Wait. What?

I'm not tryna' get all spiritual on you here, but having an open mind helps with this sort of thing. As Mary Kay Ash has put it most beautifully, "what you believe, you can achieve." As a group, we humans spend waaaay too much time focusing on what we *don't* want, and in my opinion, it's keeping more of us from achieving our life goals than we may realize. Manifestation isn't a magic trick, but it can (and does) work if you practice it regularly. If it's part of your natural day, if it's something you re-program into your mind. I want you to start trying this more often.

Manifestation is sort of like ensuring that you have a "glass half full" attitude at all times. Instead of assuming that, yes, something negative is definitely going to happen, practice anticipating that something great it going to happen instead. (P.S., This is the only time in life it's okay to assume.)

My husband and I got to a point in our late twenties

---

5 "Manifestation." Merriam-Webster.com. Merriam-Webster, n.d. Web. 16 May 2018.

where we'd start to anticipate that if something bad could *potentially* happen to us, it would. In literally any situation, we'd be completely un-surprised when something didn't go our way, and we thought it was just "us" but in hindsight, I think we were both manifesting this negative energy.

If we had to go to the passport office to get our passports updated, we'd both be anticipating that it was going to be crazy busy and that we were going to have to spend hours waiting for service. And every time we'd go, that's what would happen.

If we wanted a close parking spot at a shopping centre, we'd both be thinking, *there aren't going to be any good spots*, and then surprise! When we'd arrive, we'd get the last remaining crappy space, in the back, beside someone who apparently doesn't realize their car is supposed to be *centred* between the lines.

If we participated in any type of lottery or draw, when the tickets were getting called, all we would be thinking was "we aren't going to win. How could we possibly win? The odds are against us."

If we made plans to do something outside a week in advance, we'd both be thinking, *it's probably going to rain*, because of course something bad would happen to us.

We kept thinking in this way, and (small) shitty things would continue to happen. There's no proof or science behind this, but in the years since we've begun to work on changing our minds, I don't notice things like this happening nearly as much, if at all. I'm not saying you can simply just manifest the fact that you have the winning lottery ticket, or that someone is going to hand you buttloads of money tomorrow... I'm just saying it certainly doesn't help to be thinking about the negative option all the time. You might as well assume something positive will happen, instead.

Most recently we were on a boat trip and approaching our next overnight mooring location. As we were coming into port, on a Saturday afternoon, (quite possibly the busiest time to try to find a space to stay overnight), I stood on the bow of the boat and visualized a big, beautiful, open dock space, with a boat pulling out just as soon as we arrived. I visualized it over and over again, and repeated the phrase "big, beautiful, open dock space" in my mind.

When we showed up, as soon as we were making our way into the channel, two boats pulled out in the same place and a big, beautiful, open dock space revealed itself. I looked back at my husband and he had a big, beautiful, open smile on his face. Call it what you will, but in that moment, I believe I manifested that minor blessing through visualization and a secure belief that there would be what I wanted available, right when I wanted it.

Nobody will know for sure, but what have you got to lose? If you're always thinking negative things will happen to you, if you're always thinking you'll never get/do/have X, if you're convincing yourself you will never accomplish anything, including making lifestyle changes... as Henry Ford says: "Whether you think you can or think you can't, you're right."

What you think is your own reality. Why not practice thinking with a glass-half-full perspective?

Let's parlay this valuable knowledge to our own mindsets. It's time to focus on the positive, instead of the negative. It's time to stop thinking our legs are too fat, and start thinking our legs are strong and powerful. It's time to start telling your belly pooch that you love and appreciate it, instead of looking at it with disgust. It's time to start being grateful for broad shoulders, or thin lips, or an uneven skin tone; it's time to start swapping your negative connotations about anything you consider a "limitation", a "negative attribute" or an "insecurity" and begin to embrace these things for what they are. *Change your mind* about your body. I said *change*, dammit!

Now, adjusting your mind and your "default mode" thinking is technically easy to do, but it takes some time and some training. It's a re-programming of sorts. It doesn't happen overnight, but it does happen. We all have limiting beliefs, insecurities, negative thoughts, doubts, worries, and feelings. It's okay to have those things. Everybody does. We've been conditioned to believe we aren't good enough and need every product and workout plan and tummy-control underwear going in order to fulfill the stereotype of what a "beautiful woman" is supposed to look like. But often, they become the majority of our thoughts, instead of a one-off second guess, or an occasional musing. Acknowledging the feeling, whether it's nice or difficult, is the very first step. When you become aware of those feelings, you can better determine what to do next, instead of just ending with a negative thought and then continuing along your ~~merry~~ sad way.

What you need to do, like your life depends on it, is not allow the negative things to take up the bulk of your brain space. You are the only gatekeeper to what your mind thinks. So keep those thoughts clean and positive, would ya?

Right now, what do you automatically believe about your body? What are your autopilot thoughts, right now? What are your default-mode thought patterns that repeat like a soundtrack in your mind on a daily basis, **right now**?

Do you believe it is beautiful? Do you believe it is sexy? Strong? Powerful? Wise? Happy? Content? Graceful? ...Confident? Or are you doubtful about your beliefs? Are you wishy-washy about the things you believe about your body? If I asked you to declare how you felt in front of a mass audience, what would it sound like?

"…I guess I'm kinda strong."

"…I'm sexy sometimes, in the dark, with the best lingerie for my body type."

"…I think I'm pretty happy."

We all need to quit being so sheepish and quiet about our strengths and have stronger beliefs that empower our minds to be confident with who we are. I want you to be SO DAMN SURE of your thoughts that you would scream them in the middle of Times Square without a single care that anybody else would judge or question or debate you. If you live in Canada, you can scream them from Yonge/Dundas Square.

Right now.

Right this second.

Even if our body were to be in the state it's in NOW, forever.

At a recent speaking event where I was a panelist on balancing motherhood and self-love, another speaker was talking about positive self-talk and how you think about yourself on a daily basis, and to prove a point about how most women lack confidence, she asked the entire room (of about 100 women) "How many of you get up every single morning, look in the mirror, and have radiating confidence and feelings of self-love?"

Ninety percent of the audience kept their hands down, dropped their eyes low and nodded shamefully. Ten percent hemmed and hawed and looked around the room first before sheepishly lifting their arm half way up. I raised my hand immediately and kept it high in the air, at the risk of looking "conceited."

The room laughed at the irony of this, of course, but then I chimed in. I wasn't attempting to negate the other speaker's point (because she was right, for the most part, assuming nobody would have raised their hands), but I wanted to be clear that part of the problem, in addition to us needing work on self-acceptance and confidence in the current climate of our Western culture influences, is that we've been taught our whole lives not to be conceited. It's easier to fit in and self-loathe and pick yourself apart and talk about what you don't like about yourself, than to shine bright and share what you think rocks about yourself. Because probably around the time you were a pre-teen, it was socially unacceptable or negative to be "conceited." I remember that very clearly in elementary school. I would hear my friends talk about another girl with a negative connotation if someone appeared conceited. So what do you think I did from that moment on? I allowed other people's judgement or assessment of me dictate how I responded to things. I kept my hand down. I had a hard time coming up with positive things that I liked about myself. I didn't dare share openly if I *gasp* thought I looked good in my new jeans. Heaven forbid someone talk about themselves in a positive way. I would think constantly, "Oops! Don't say that, it'll come across like you're conceited!" Society tells us "OMG! Love yourself! Accept yourself! Embrace your body!" but then in almost the same sentence it says "Woah—not THAT much... you conceited betch!"

Luckily, there is a difference between confidence and conceit. It's difficult to decipher, though, as a teenager who is just desperately hoping to fit in, conform, and connect with other teenagers. Self-loathing becomes an adolescent connection strategy that trickles into adulthood and it's like poison. But, there is a difference between self-assurance and cockiness. Acceptance and ego. One is quiet and respectful, one is loud and abrupt. I didn't realize this as a pre-teen. So, I was conditioned. Over and over. Repeating the same behaviours. Which left me second guessing myself and self-loathing, even while no-one was looking, alone as a grown adult. I questioned my abilities and skills. I doubted my worth and value, and hated my appearance. These beliefs led me to quietly overtrain, and do things like go to a tanning bed every other day, take fat-burning pills, do every diet under the sun, dye my hair, wear cool clothes... at the pursuit of fitting in socially. We do these things, but never actually talk about feeling good about ourselves. "Don't be cocky!" "Don't be conceited!"

To punctuate my point, I shared an example from the movie Mean Girls, naturally. Most of the audience got the reference. There was one lady in the back who didn't look too enthused, but whatevs. There's a scene where Cady Heron (Lindsay Lohan) is in Regina George's room and all three of the "Plastics" are standing around casually talking about the traits they don't like about themselves. While standing together in front of a full-length mirror, Karen says her hips are huge. Gretchen joins and says she hates her calves. Regina says she can't wear halter tops because she has "man shoulders." Gretchen says her hairline is weird. Regina says her pores are huge. Karen says her nail beds suck. Cady doesn't know what to say in order to fit in, so she musters "Um. I have really bad breath in the morning" and none of the girls seem to be satisfied with her obviously forced complaint.

The culture we live in supports self-loathing over self-loving, and it has become a form of connection between women to share the things they're not happy with. Maybe it's so we don't look conceited. Maybe it's so we get sympathy and objection from our friends, who do not typically see us in the negative-coloured lens through which we see ourselves. Maybe it's so we fit in with everyone else who is talking shit about themselves, instead of being the odd woman out and proclaiming your undying love for your own self, unapologetically, in a group of people who are unhappy, struggle to fit the mould, and have pre-conceived expectations about the negativity around being "conceited."

I don't have all the answers, but I do know that more women should be able to raise their hands confidently, without fearing others think they're being conceited, when asked the question: "Do you get up every morning and feel good about yourself?"

What do you say? Could you be happy with the you that exists right here and now? Because that's the only body you've got, my friend. There's far more to you than just your exterior shell, and you also aren't required to fall in love with every single bit of yourself, all at once, immediately. This shit takes time, so let's re-work that mindset, embrace ourselves the best we can now, work on loving even just a few pieces of the person we are in this exact moment, without expecting her to change in any way. That's the goal, anyway.

#MOMFIDENTAF

"There is a difference between self-assurance and cockiness. Acceptance and ego. One is quiet and respectful, the other is loud and abrupt."

Chapter Eight
ASSESSING PIVOTAL MOMENTS

At some point in my young adult life, I officially decided that I "hated my arms." Actually, scratch that vague sentiment. I can pinpoint when *exactly* I came to this decision. I was about 21 and working as an entry-level manager in that same gym where I had humble customer service beginnings. My superior was hella passionate about fitness and had previously done several "fitness competitions". Pardon the parentheses, but I am not a fan of the "sport" of fitness competing. I know there are people who love them and who will continue to participate in them, and my advice to those people is to continue to do what makes them happy. But there's so much that goes into this highly restrictive, unsustainable, and unrealistic lifestyle that I personally feel it is mentally and emotionally damaging, in addition to actually being physically damaging to your body systems. Throw in the fact that the "sport" is based solely on the judgement of a body aesthetic and how someone "looks" compared directly to how someone else looks, and I think it's a very unhealthy version of sport. Of course, this is my opinion and to anyone who is an active part of that community, I mean no disrespect. You may fully disagree with me. That's cool. We can still be friends despite agreeing to disagree!

Anyway, my superior and I were in a meeting discussing something challenging about the results of the previous month's sales performance. And because it was such a stressful, difficult month, I hadn't worked out that much throughout it. Apparently, she noticed. She urged me to consider how I was implementing fitness into my weekly routine, and get back to my training sessions. It was lovely of her to care about my fitness level, and I agreed, but immediately felt ashamed, guilty, and also confused as to why she was bringing this up. She asked about my fitness goals. I obliged by saying what most women say on cue to that question, something like, "Oh, I want to lose 20 pounds." She nodded.

"Yeah. You carry a LOT of weight in your arms."

Um. Thanks for noticing? I wasn't sure how to respond to her comment. I couldn't argue, I had never really paid much attention before, but now that she'd pointed it out, I *did* seem to have fatty arms, didn't I? UGH. What a shitty person I must be, walking around with these horrible fat arms. Excuse me, I need to go workout immediately. Great meeting.

How did she expect me to respond?

As it turns out, I didn't say anything, I just felt tears well up in my eyes and spun my wheel-y chair around so I was out of view and she couldn't see me crying. I felt embarrassed. Ashamed. Guilty. Fat. Like a fraud. My self-esteem plummeted a few points that day. As a normal, healthy, tall young woman living in a larger frame, I had already regularly engaged in self-hate, self-loathing, and self-judgement of various parts of my body in the past, and I now had a brand new body part to throw shade to.

Thanks a LOT.

I can appreciate that her comment was *likely* born out of a place of love, and caring, and a deep-rooted urge to help me, considering her background in fitness and what her personal expectations were of how someone lives a fit life. She wanted me to take care of myself, but it came out in a really harsh way. Maybe I was too sensitive. Maybe she didn't mean to hurt my personal feelings. To be fair, it *was* just an observation, but I took it to heart and took it personally, because I'd been taught that "fat arms" were not a good thing, so having them must definitely be a negative trait. That's the thing about body language, though. It can be damaging, even if it's just someone's cold observation. I wish I had the balls to tell her just how damaging that kind of comment is to a young woman. To any woman. It literally stuck with me since then and I, to this day, have an arm insecurity when I'm not being very careful about my words and thoughts. My arms are big, but I've now released the evaluation that "big" equals "bad." That feels good. Big does not equal bad.

That situation aside, I want you to realize that there may be pivotal moments in your life where something changed for you. Maybe a parent, or a school bully, or a colleague, or a relative, or even someone who you thought was a very good friend, said something uncalled for that made you switch gears completely in the arena of how you think about yourself. It has the potential to shift your entire life from that moment on, and unfortunately, if you're reading this, I'm sure these moments have already happened to you and have affected you completely, so we can't avoid it happening. But we can do some work around it now.

Maybe you were in an awkward stage and had grown wider before you grew taller, and Aunt Sally decided to comment that you, "Certainly haven't been missing any meals, have you?"

PIVOT.

Maybe you were in the throes of your first year of college, had a shitty soccer game, and your dad made a seemingly innocent comment about how you'd be quicker on the ball if you lost the 10 pounds you gained so far during freshman year.

PIVOT.

Maybe you overheard your grandparents arguing about who ate the last of the cookies, and then someone accused you of being the culprit, because, well, you're the "bigger" one of the cousin group, naturally.

PIVOT.

(I really hope you're picturing Ross Gellar right now. If you aren't, you're missing out on how you view the word *pivot* for the rest of your life. 100%.)

There may be a distinctive moment, or a collection of moments, that have contributed to how you feel about yourself, how your insecurities have been conceived, and how you carry yourself now because of it. I'll never forget hearing an uncle tell me, while I was about nine-years-old eating probably the last Oreo from the sleeve I'd inhaled, that "cookies go straight to the hips." Back then, I didn't really feel it affected me, but is it any coincidence I remember that moment to this day? I remember where I was sitting. I remember what cookies I was eating. I remember where he was standing. I remember the colour of the room, and specific design of the wallpaper. (It was 1997, every room had wallpaper.)

I remember every detail. And while it may be true that often these comments come from a place of love, and aren't actually meant to do harm, it doesn't negate the fact that it can be harmful and damaging to a young girl (or boy, for that matter). I know with certainty that this uncle did not mean to cause me any internal damage or hurt my feelings. I know he didn't think twice about what he said because he didn't think there was anything wrong with it. It was light. It was meant to be funny. He laughed afterwards. I sure as hell know he didn't think that measly comment would have stuck with me for the rest of my life. I know this in my bones.

An adult sees a child inhaling cookies like it's their job, and they are probably just naturally concerned that the child doesn't realize cookies are not good for them. At nine-years-old, I was also one of those kids that got wider before she got taller, so I was going through a visible expansion phase. So the adult makes a comment to combat the behaviour, casually. But it can be damaging, because instead of saying "Did you know cookies aren't really that good for you? They're okay sometimes, but they don't really have any nutrients! Here, wanna split an apple with me?" it comes out like, "you're going to get fat if you eat that cookie. And being fat is quite possibly the worst thing you could ever do to yourself EVER, you know that right?" There's a difference, no? It's harder and more complicated and takes more work and effort and thought to say the former. It's easier to just say "Cookies make you fat. Don't eat those." And I'm not saying that adults should beat around the bush about things; I'm just saying that a more careful effort about the way we use our language around impressionable kids - both girls and boys - is important.

Moments can define us. And you may have a multitude of difficult moments saved up from your life that have all slowly contributed to how you feel about yourself in general. But the truth is, you are the only one who can impact how you feel about yourself, what you think about yourself, and how you carry yourself. Nobody else is going to change your mind about how you feel. YOU have to put in the work to change that. (I mean, maaaaybe a book with some mildly inspiring and practical self-acceptance advice from an external source can help too. I dunno. You tell me. *wink*) The hard fact is **nobody else is responsible for your self-acceptance.** You can choose to do the work, to pay attention, to shift your perspective and to become okay with yourself as you are, or you can allow the collection of pivotal moments, comments, and negative nay-sayers to shape how you think about yourself for the rest of your life. I don't expect you to forget about them completely; if you went though some very difficult times, were bullied in school, or continue to have a difficult time due to external sources throwing shady energy at you, that shit is a heightened challenge to manage, and I feel for you, don't get me wrong. But my argument remains: **You** are the only one who has control over what you're thinking and thus feeling about yourself. **You** are the only one who can make a difference to your environment, what you expose yourself to, and who you surround yourself with. And the good news is, with regular practice and focus, you can shift your thoughts. You can shift your exposure. You can change your environment. You can edit your circle. It's a journey, a process, and takes dedication, but it is absolutely possible.

I'll spare you the spiritual woo-woo bullshit, for now. The point is, the way you speak to yourself could quite possibly be the most important language you facilitate, monitor, and execute in your entire life. Even more than what other people say about or to you. Even more than what you say to others, and yet we tend to be *much* easier on others than we are on ourselves.

#MOMFIDENTAF

"Nobody else is responsible for your own self-acceptance."

Chapter Nine

UNICORN SELF-LOVE ASSISTANTS

Imagine for a moment that your best friend is getting married. She's in the middle of trying on the sexiest form-fitting gown you've ever seen, when she starts to break down in tears. At first, you think they might be happy tears, but then you realize she's having a breakdown because she thinks her arms look huge and her back somehow has "fat" that's showing. (Maybe an old boss created this perception for her, who the hell knows.) These things she thinks about herself were things that had *neh-ver* crossed your mind. Not once. You were in fact just admiring how beautiful her silhouette looked in that off-white colour, and were silently wishing you had her collarbones and could pull off a naked-shoulder look like she could. You never even thought for a second that there were anything wrong with her arms or back. So you console her. You talk her off the ledge. You hug it out and she stops crying and starts laughing instead. You tell her all the wonderful, beautiful things about her, the things you love, the things you were just silently admiring, and you make her feel like the most beautiful woman in the world.

The problem with this example is that as women, we're often the person trying on the proverbial wedding dress, and we're also often the ones shaming ourselves or complaining about a body part. But then there's nobody there to help console us. And there won't be… unless you have some kind of unicorn self-love assistant who casually sits around with champagne and tells you beautiful things about yourself every day. (If you do, I'd like her number please!) That's not happening anytime soon, so instead, we have to take on the role of "Unicorn Self-Love Assistant" and feed ourselves with the positive comments instead of believing the negative ones. Congratulations, you're hired. No experience necessary.

Your mind will believe what you tell it. If you keep telling it negative things, it is bound to start believing them. Think about that for a second. If you keep thinking to yourself, "I hate my body, I hate my body, I hate my body," why *wouldn't* your brain be pre-programmed to believe that it is unworthy, unlovable, unfit, unhealthy, and not capable of doing anything good for you? Why *wouldn't* your self-image be incessantly nasty, judgemental and pre-disposed to negativity? Whatever you're thinking in your mind is what your mind is going to believe. The more you can start practicing positive thoughts (and words, eventually), the more your brain will take on whatever those thoughts are.

So, if you replace "I hate my body" with "I love my strong legs" instead, eventually, that's what your mind is going to believe by default. But it can't happen until you at least attempt to start making a brain-change. Lather those good thoughts. Really *feel* them. Then rinse and repeat. Outside of *thinking* good things about yourself, your body, and your overall worth, it'll be waaay more beneficial if you start saying things *out loud*. Now, don't get me wrong. I used to think saying things out loud (AKA, affirmations) was a bit of a crock, too. So if you're a bit skeptical, that's okay. It took me a while to embrace them, but I'm seriously thrilled that I wound up sticking to it. Here's the deal. Affirmations are really easy to do. Technically, you don't need anything to start incorporating your own affirmation-type mantras into your day to day life. I do find that using affirmation cards are helpful, especially at the beginning. (Sidebar: My favourite affirmation cards are from Love Powered Co. They're beautiful, they're inspiring, and there's a specific version for women, teens, and littles. Brilliant.)

Using a physical tool means that you don't even have to think about it, and you can have the deck to not only remind you with a literal, physical, visible reference to do affirmations, but to actually have something to say if you can't think of anything to start.

Now, listen. I am well aware that creating a positive self-image is far easier said than done. It doesn't happen overnight. It involves lots of thought work, intentional practice, and choosing to see things in a different way. I can also attest to the fact that building this kind of body positivity is even more difficult after you become a mother. Bodies are stretched and squeezed and challenged and tested in ways they never have been before, and somehow we're supposed to just jump right back into life, take care of a tiny human, and be okay with a body that's sometimes drastically different than it used to be. Sometimes, external changes are difficult to deal with, physically and mentally, and that's okay. But it can't rule your life forever.

Self-love is a personal responsibility. Nobody else can love you enough for you to love yourself. You can't rely on your partner, parents, siblings, or anyone else to take responsibility for helping you to love your own *self*. It's an inside job. An important one. It isn't up to anyone else to fight for, navigate, or figure out. I wish I had a unicorn self-love assistant that spoke positively to me twenty-four/seven. Unfortunately, I don't, and it's unrealistic to hope for someone else to do the positive thinking for you, anyway. Unicorn or not. It has to start with you and grow with you.

Have you ever had one of those debilitating change room moments, where you step into that tiny room with high hopes, but on this particular day nothing is fitting right, your usual size is too tight, the pants you picked that looked like they'd fit aren't making it past your knees, and the only thing you notice is any potential flaw, imperfection, or side boob that is apparently glaring and poignant? What happens during this episode? Do you give yourself a hug and say, "It's okay, you're okay, you are not defined by this and you're a beautiful person, no matter what the tags say"? Or do you allow this one moment to let you spiral out of control into an entire day, week, or month of self-deprecating thoughts and behaviours that make you feel even worse? I don't know about you, but I've definitely done the latter, multiple times. This one, seemingly small life task (trying on new clothes) somehow has the potential to unravel us depending on if the tag goes up or down. Please remember, always, that you are a fluctuating human being and size is irrelevant to worth. It may not feel like that right now, but I promise you, there is nothing more valuable about a person who is a size four than a person who is a size twenty. The issue is that society, generally, makes it clear that they prefer the smaller size. And while there is nothing wrong with *any* woman, at *any* size, it's unfair that we torture ourselves based on the assumption that when it comes to your value as a human being, you measure it based on a "*less* body is more *value*" distinction.

#MOMFIDENTAF

"Your mind will believe whatever you tell it. If you keep telling it negative things, it is bound to start believing them."

Chapter Ten

MOVEMENT MATTERS

I can't talk about confidence without talking about fitness. Why? Because feeling good about yourself starts with the inside, and fitness, my dear friend, is primarily for the inside. Marketing and advertising in the fitness industry has taught us that working out is primarily for shaping the outside. That's backwards.

A long, long time ago (like, I'm talking 70-80 bajillion years ago[6]) humans needed to move their bodies physically every day in order to survive. They hunted, they gathered, they basically spent their entire lives trying to avoid danger and source food. And that meant they moved their bodies A LOT. No real transportation outside of maaaaybe a horse and their own two feet,

---

6   Approximate figure, naturally

meant they needed to be active if they wanted to go anywhere. (Just imagine how many steps they'd acquire if we strapped a Fitbit on 'em!) Our current society has changed so much. Not just in the more convenient way that we obtain our food, but in the plethora of food items available and invented every day. A lot of those foods aren't even "real", but have chemical ingredients invented over time and often added to preserve the food so it lasts longer on the supermarket shelves. You better believe 70,000 years ago, they weren't keeping their foraged food for long, they were just eating it and then finding the next perishable food. There wasn't really such thing as "non-perishable" back then.

Food acquisition aside, our culture has also shifted to become dramatically more sedentary. Technology has created jobs where people don't even have to leave their houses. Not only are we sitting all day, but we don't even have to do the incredibly basic commute to get from our homes to our jobs, which mitigates a whole lot of daily movement, if you add it all up. We also have apps for everything: to deliver our food, to find us a hotel, to connect with friends and family, to tell us the weather, to meet people before we date them... we basically don't need to move at all and can accomplish a lot from the palm of our hands. This is very cool, but is also increasingly harmful. Getting regular movement for our bodies (that were created for movement in order to survive, remember) is becoming less and less of a priority for many people. Because our jobs are often very inactive, we need to make it a point to move our bodies whenever we can. And as you'll see, I don't mean you need to torture yourself with two-a-days or become a marathon runner (unless of course you *want* to...), but you **do need** movement in some way, shape, or form. I am an advocate for you to make your own decisions in life, that best suit you and your needs, your circumstances, and your lifestyle, but I'm also a believer that every single human being on this earth needs to move their body regularly. You can quote me on that. If you're a size two or a size twenty-two, you need movement. It's not about your body aesthetic, muscle tone, or weight loss. It's about strength, stability, maintenance, and taking care of yourself so your body functions at an optimal level for you on a daily basis. That's literally it.

Remember when I asked you if you'd be happy with your body as it is *right now*? And if you'd continue to workout and eat well, even if there were no physical changes possible? Ideally, your answer would be that you are happy with your body in its current state, and that you *would* still workout, even if there were no potential physical changes. But… I have a feeling that isn't the case for many moms and women out there. There are many benefits to fitness, but I think most of us on this earth connect losing weight with looking good, and in order to lose weight (so that we look good) we must be working out, and so that's typically the main motivator. That's okay for the short term, but you need to understand why fitness is about so much more than just what you look like on the outside. It's not your fault if you think that way; we've been told our entire lives that fitness = lose weight = look good. But it's not about that. It's about rewarding and thanking our bodies, not for punishing and torturing it, like it's done something wrong. But, I know. Working out is hard. It's physically difficult, it takes up time in your day and week, it (can) require special clothing and equipment, it makes you sweaty and a little less "presentable", making it difficult to squeeze in before you go anywhere, and it's one more thing you have to execute, accomplish, and coordinate in your busy life. I know, I know, I KNOW!

So I would *not* be surprised if you'd forego finding time for exercise if there were literally no aesthetic benefits possible. Exercise is so great for WAY MORE than just the external appearance, but I think it's pretty clear that everybody enjoys the ultimate side-effects from activity that can include losing weight, toning up, fitting into your clothes better and just in general, looking and feeling fucking badass and incredible. Right?

Okay, so, there are clearly benefits to working out that can affect your physical appearance, and in turn, that can affect your confidence. (Duh.) Isn't that *exciting* though!? We do live in a world where making changes to diet and exercise can impact our outward appearance! We *do* have the option to curate our fitness and with consistency, see and feel results that can change our bodies for the better! We do have the chance to take our health into our own hands and impact it in incredible ways by incorporating fitness into our lives! We *aren't* stuck with the same body forever, and we *can* decide to make real changes anytime we want! That's amazing! The really important distinction to make is that you do not need to hold yourself accountable to using fitness to change yourself. You can release the expectation that hitting the gym three days a week should warrant visible changes by any specific timeline. Yes, it's a bonus that I think we'd all receive, but what if you decided to move your body during the week so you *felt* great, instead of looked great? What if you released the expectation that you're "trying to lose twenty pounds" and just considered movement something you do because it's important, like brushing your teeth or getting an oil change? (Real quick, let this be your reminder to book an oil change. You're overdue for one, aren't you? I knew it. Oil changes are supposed to be preventative and regular, not sporadic, reactive, and overdue. When your car has some kind of massive, expensive issue, it's likely because you didn't take care of it preventatively with regular maintenance. Consider movement the oil change of your body. If you don't want yourself to blow up later, get moving regularly. Go call your mechanic now. You're welcome. Sincerely, my husband is a mechanic.)

Listen to me, sweet mama. If you take just one thing from this chapter, please let it be this:

Exercise > Appearance

Exercise is far more important for you to maintain, on a regular and somewhat consistent basis, than appearing skinny ever will be. It is far more important to create a habit of movement for alllllllll the things it can accomplish *inside* your body, not only for what change it can produce outside your body. Unfortunately for your self-esteem, society has this backwards. So much of the advertising for fitness and exercise is focused on what you *look like*, or rather, what you *should* look like, and not on the actual physical and intrinsic benefits that fitness can provide.

Let me just remind you, the fitness industry would not exist if everybody were running around, exercising on their own for the joy of movement, loving their bodies at any size and not caring if they "should" look "better" than they currently do. The fitness industry *wants* you to have a crappy body image. They don't want you to walk into their gym and be like "I'm already really happy with myself!" That's not as good leverage for closing a membership sale than "I'm really unhappy and need to lose twenty pounds so I feel good about myself *sad face*" When you aren't accepting of your current circumstances, you're more likely to feel pressure to measure up, compare yourself to all the photoshopped and airbrushed bodies you see in LITERALLY EVERY ADVERTISEMENT EVER, and think the only answer is to pay money to buy something that'll help you *make* your body fit into the proverbial box. Fitness, in the developed world, has become an industry. It's literally "the promotion of goods or related services within an economy." It's an industry with strong morals and healthy roots, sure, but it's also an industry that wants to make money, honey. Hence why there are so many ridiculous products on the market that are marketed to make us think we need them in order to look a certain way. This is confusing because, fitness, exercise, movement, whatever you call it - is inherently good. We DO need fitness in our lives, like I said firmly at the start. I stand by that. We need to prioritize it and move every day if possible. But we *don't* need strict rules, guidelines, crazy programs, expensive equipment or clothes, a six-pack, visible traps, 10% body fat, or to obsessively train for the sole purpose of fitting into a body ideal box that is unrealistic for many people. The pressure to conform to that expected image is suffocating.

It's hard to separate sometimes, but just know this:

you don't *need* any "products" to live a fit and healthy life. You don't even need any fitness equipment. You can use your body, you can use any resistance you have around you (like, a certain twenty-pound baby, or fifty-pound four-year-old maybe?) and you can get all your meals from real food and not from nutritional (expensive and sometimes questionable) meal replacement shakes. That's just my opinion.

See also: anything a Kardashian promotes is not something you want or need. You'll survive without it.

Here is a quick roundup of just a few incredible benefits of getting regular movement, in case you forgot or are still heavily brainwashed that movement is for the sole purpose of weight loss. Regular exercise helps you build muscle strength, (and maintain that strength for everyday tasks like, I don't know, picking up those carseats and toddlers?) Regular movement helps you build bone density, improve balance, improve sleep, improve mood, give you more energy, improve cardiovascular and respiratory systems, improve and increase your metabolism, improve agility, improve focus, improve flexibility, build brain and cognitive health, and create a positive mindset about yourself, your ability, and your body that is difficult to achieve if you don't practice finding out what said body is capable of. Of this, I am *sure*. And all of those things are benefits that you can't actually see. There are WAY more benefits to a regular fitness program than what you or even other people can notice. In fact, when starting a fitness program, you're guaranteed to immediately notice a difference in the way you *feel*, even though you don't see any actual physical changes. True story. You know this if you've been at all active in the past. Even if I'm having the most horrible, body-negative day, as soon as I incorporate exercise into my day, I do a complete 180 degree attitude adjustment. Even if nothing has happened to my body (because literally nothing has changed in weight, shape, size, measurement…) I feel 100% better, stronger, more focused, and happier than I did pre-movement. I dare you to try doing a workout and feeling bad about yourself after.

***

Imagine you could have $500,000 in your bank account in 6 months, or you could have $10,000 in $1 bills right now. When you can see, feel, and touch the bills in real time, right away, it seems like they're more important and valuable. But the money in the bank, that you cannot see or touch, is worth literally 50 TIMES the money in front of you. It's easy to get wrapped up with the stuff that's right in front of you. Think about exercise as being as beneficial as the invisible (but real!) $500,000 in the bank. Eventually, you'll be able to take out $10,000 in real cash, if you want to, but the stuff in the bank is the most important, most valuable stuff, and you can't even see a damn dime of it.

Did I make my point? *Sips coffee*

Thinking about exercise with only the end goal of "looking good" in mind is dangerous. It allows you to quit sooner, when you don't "see" results fast enough. It makes you think you aren't successful if you don't lose a certain amount of pounds. The main objective of fitness is for the long-term health benefits you will gain (the $500,000), not the short term external "looking good" drive (the $10,000). We need to spend our energy learning how to **make fitness a habit**, with less focus on the exact program you follow, and more focus on actually doing something *regularly*. It's like spending all your time wrapped up with the outside cover of a book, thinking about how good it does or does not look, and never dedicating the time to digesting all the good stuff that's inside. The content, the words, the pages, the stories, the ideas, the concepts... that's the good stuff. That's the beneficial stuff. That's the stuff that will really change you. Not the outside cover.

So, of course, exercise is important. For more reasons than one. This much is clear. But *what* you're doing, doesn't matter quite as much. This is where you'll need to hear me out. The exercise program that's going to work for you, so you can get results, feel strong, create a habit, embrace exercise for life, and improve your overall health in multiple ways (including perhaps losing weight, if that's part of the goal)... is the one that you're going to actually DO. We already discussed that exercise is hard. It's hard to fit into your routine, it can be boring, it is physically challenging and it makes you sweaty and ruins your hair. How rude! So in order to see any results from exercise, the key requirement is that you actually DO the workout. The only way you're going to actually do it, is if you actually ENJOY it.

EXAMPLE 1: NON-SUSTAINABLE RESULT

It's January 1st. You're motivated to drop some pounds. You find a health-guru online and decide to follow their specific and intense fitness plan that promises if you follow their plan exactly, you'll get "ripped abs" and "lose 20 pounds in 6 days!" Woo-hoo!

You workout for 90 minutes every day for that first week. You pack your gym bag, you drink your shakes, you meal prep, you go to the gym at 6am before work, and you post about how you "didn't miss a workout!" that entire week. #GymLife #FitFam #NoExcuses

The next week you're tired from putting in so much effort. You hit the gym on Monday, and Tuesday, and then decide to skip it on Wednesday. You try again on Thursday and then feel like taking the weekend off, because you've worked so hard, naturally. You deserve a break.

By week three you begin justifying why taking it

easy is necessary for you right now. You're tired. You're swamped at work. You want to sleep in, your body *needs* the extra sleep. You don't want to go to the gym after work because that's family time. You can't workout at home. You don't feel like grocery shopping. You can't maintain this crazy workout schedule, so why bother trying at all? You go back to the gym one more day, and then forget about all the extra work required and don't get back there until several months later. But you don't stick with it that time, either. You don't see results and you believe getting what you want is unattainable.

Total time spent intentionally moving your body over the year: about 15 hours.

EXAMPLE 2: SUSTAINABLE RESULT

Let's now consider if it's January 1st, and you don't set any crazy outrageous fitness or weight loss goals, but you instead decide that moving your body is going to be a priority for you this year, because it matters to you at a cellular level. You want to keep up with your kids, teach them how to enjoy movement, and plan to use your gym sessions as "me time" for your own mental health. You snag a set of dumbbells and decide you're going to move your body for twenty minutes a day, three times per week. You start trekking down the path of creating a habit. ONE habit. Movement every week.

The first week, you feel like you aren't doing enough and it almost seems too easy, but you've found a great place in your spare bedroom for your workouts, and you've come up with a plan to do it first thing in the morning after you brush your teeth on Monday, Wednesday and Friday.

You have kids, so you need to make sure you do quick and effective workouts so you can get it done in those precious, sacred, and important twenty minutes. You don't worry about what you look like, sometimes you wear your pyjamas, and you don't follow a specific program, you just do body weight moves with added resistance of the dumbbells. You follow Pinterest workout plans and YouTube videos.

Six months in, and you've gotten three twenty minute workout sessions per week without much difficulty. It has now become a habit that you don't want to miss. You notice how good it makes you feel, and how integral that alone time is for you. It makes you a better mom; you are prioritizing yourself so that you can then prioritize others with a full tank and lots of energy. You don't feel pressure or forced to workout; it's important to you, so you do it. You feel more energetic, you're sleeping better, you bounce out of bed in the morning, and you have no problem running around with your kids without getting out of breath. You have lost a few pounds, your clothes are fitting better and you can even notice some definition in your arms from lifting your weights.

You are no longer focused on achieving an external goal, nor are you motivated by seeing visible results, but you've created a habit that is easy to maintain and that you feel good about. Your workouts may be short, but they're effective and consistent.

You keep this habit up for the entire year.

Total time spent intentionally moving your body over the year: about 48 hours.

Conclusion: movement becoming a habit is more important than the exact program you follow. Small, incremental progress is far superior to going hard out of the gates and then losing momentum and subsequently giving up. Sustainability is quite possibly the most important factor after habit when it comes to movement. If you can't keep up your workout schedule for the rest of your life, you may need to re-think it.

The right movement strategy for you is the one that includes exercise you enjoy and can upkeep on a regular basis. What do you *truly* enjoy doing? For me, for a very long time, it was fitness classes. I loved working out in a team environment, with loud, motivating music. My love for it drew me to become a fitness instructor when I was eighteen, and I loved pushing other people to reach their fitness goals and keep them interested and engaged in their workout. I loved the programs and the movements and the environment. I found that my favourite part was helping others find a way to love fitness; a way to keep coming back and maintain their healthy habit. If they loved it, they'd return. I freaking *loved* it, and it became a regular, consistent and habitual part of my life, and that, in turn, helped me see natural results.

I also found solace in running, and as I grew into my third decade, I realized I enjoy it in part for the exercise, but also in part for the solidarity of being by myself, listening to music, not talking, and just experiencing the environment. (Or, the treadmill. Sometimes it's not possible to run outside. Like literally, Canada is snowy AF for like 7 months of the year.) I realized this only when we got a dog. The idea of running with your pooch was like a dream come true for me. When I started running with him, all I was doing was getting frustrated, telling him to "HEEL! HEEL! FUCKING HEEL! DAMMIT!!!!!" I also had to modify my pace or stance because someone else was coming with a dog and I'd have to move off the sidewalk... so needless to say, after a few jaunts with the pooch, I decided running was *my* thing. I don't like running with a buddy. I don't like running while pushing a stroller. I don't like talking or policing while I'm running, and it's actually more about being by myself, supporting my mental health, and honoring my need for alone time, than it is about getting active. So you need to ask yourself, what's your "thing" and how can you do it more?

Plain and simple, results come from consistent effort. And, yes, results can also come from quick, intense, short term effort (like following a strict plan), but *lasting* results, the kind that keep you motivated for the rest of your life, *lasting* results come from consistent effort. If you want to be consistent, you better at least enjoy it a little bit. Or else, guess what? You'll quit. If the only option was to run with my dog, I'd have quit by now. Make the changes you need to make so the circumstances work for you, and maintain. Rinse and repeat. Make it so important to you that even when obstacles arise, you *want* to do your workout. Not because you might gain two pounds if you skip it, but because it's important to you. Not because you're obsessively exercising so you can post an insta-selfie immediately afterwards, but because it's important to you. Not because you want to squeeze into your jeans from when you were 18, but **because it's *fucking* important to you.**

So here's the scoop. Your mission is to find something that *you* truly enjoy doing. And trust me, I know, it's not easy to profess your undying "love" for a fitness program. It can be intense and difficult; it makes you sweaty and somewhat unpresentable; it takes up time in your day... but is probably the most valuable and important component or "task" that you could invest in, outside of eating well. You will also need to find a time in your day that you can accomplish your movement, whether that's first thing in the morning, three days a week, or paired nicely with your *Friends* binge on Netflix every week-night at 8pm. (One episode is about 22 minutes... just saying!) Before you even think about what you're physically going to do, find a place where you can slot this precious movement time into your day. Remember, **habit trumps details. Consistency trumps intensity. Showing up trumps specifics.**

To ensure you're getting the biggest return on investment of your time and energy for fitness, find something that incorporates all areas of fitness: cardio, strength, and flexibility. From there, do what you need to do to fit it into your life. Get into your local (convenient) gym, join a small studio, get a personal trainer, do workouts from home, use your environment, use your children... whatever works. Make sure whatever you're doing is getting your heart rate up and challenging your muscles, whether you're challenging them with resistance training or flexibility.

Aim to spend focused time on resistance training at least a few times per week. If you're an old-school "gym go-er", you might feel you need to go heavy on the cardio. That's not the case. If you have weight to lose, you still need to be lifting weights. Don't spend all your time on the treadmill. That ship has sailed, ladies. I know, I used to be a "cardio bunny" too. I'm not sure where that came from. Jane Fonda? Nobody can be sure. In any case, get off the treadmill and learn how to weight train properly. Lift moderate to heavy weights, and train your entire body. I think you know what I'm going to say next... if you're sitting there, in your Lululemon tights and your top knot and you're like: "I have no f*cking clue how to workout properly, nor do I have even a vague sense of how to navigate the gym without looking ridiculous or hurting myself" ... then find yourself a personal trainer to guide you or just start working out at *home* before you venture into a public place dedicated to sweating. The most important part is that you start. Don't make it too complicated.

For general fitness for overall health, the most efficient and effective way to do this is to incorporate strength, cardio, and flexibility into every workout. They all serve a unique, yet collaborative purpose. Setting fitness goals is an excellent practice to get into, but, again, you may need the help of someone who is trained to facilitate this type of goal setting. If you have a big weight loss goal to reach, you may need to get a bit more serious and detailed about what you're doing and how often.

Finally, if your goal is much more complex and advanced than simply maintaining an active lifestyle, toning up, slipping easier into your mom jeans or perhaps losing a few pounds, then you may need to enlist the help of a uniquely trained professional. That will always be my recommendation. If your goal is to learn how to power lift or train for a triathlon, you will likely need to follow a more advanced workout regime. I don't mean to suggest that casually playing pick-up soccer twice a week is going to help you win the top spot in your age group at your local half marathon in three months. If your goals are specific and detailed, then your workout program will likely need to be as well. So ask for help!

#MOMFIDENTAF

"Habit trumps details. Consistency trumps intensity. Showing up trumps specifics."

Chapter Eleven

YOGA SCH-MOGA

On the heels of an entire chapter about movement, I'd now like to personally grace your eyeballs with a thrilling tale about yoga. I think it's safe to say, you've heard about yoga. Right? You probably at least know about it from a physical standpoint; you've maybe tried a class or two; you may have even gotten into that crazy hot yoga fad and tried executing complicated moves in ridiculous temperatures (for some reason). Whether you've practiced the physical component of yoga, have gone deeper into the spiritual practice, know nothing or know it all, know this:

Yoga is not about your body.

Did you know that the physical postures, or "Asanas" in yoga are only *one* of a potential *eight* limbs of

Yoga Philosophy? That's right. That's like if you picture your entire body, and consider that your 2 arms, 2 legs, 1 head and 1 torso contribute to making your entire body whole. The movements or physical part of yoga represents your left arm. The entire rest of your body is all the other components that make up the thing we call "yoga", collectively. But we don't take as much time getting to know those things as we do with the physical practice. Why? Because yoga has been thrust into Western fitness culture as something that's supposed to be a "workout." And sure, yes, when practiced properly, yoga can *definitely* be a workout, in the traditional sense of the word. You *do* physically execute moves in sequence; you *do* often gain some benefit in the way of building muscle strength, building flexibility and in some cases, even raising your heart rate. But the most important part of yoga, in my opinion, is how well you are training your *mind* while diving into your practice.

When I was young and naive and officially had a gym membership at thirteen years old, I remember taking my very first "yoga" class. I had no idea what I was doing, and clearly I didn't even know how to follow the class schedule properly, because I walked into a class that I thought was "yoga" but was actually called "Pilates." That's quite a distinction, I'll have you know. The instructor didn't mention much about the class, she just instructed me to set up my mat beside another exerciser, and the class began right away.

It was intense. I was sweating. Profusely. We were crunching and rolling and using those huge exercise balls. We were moving our limbs and breathing heavy; we were getting our heart rates up; we were working our cores and our backs and our glutes and our shoulders. We were getting dedicated water breaks. We were towelling off between "sets". We were breathing heavy and there was some "woo-hoo!"-ing.

I left that class thinking: "Sh*t, yoga is HARD AF." (Well, that's a lie. "As f*ck" was not a trendy unit of measurement at that time.)

Fast-forward four years, and I found myself working the front desk of a gym. As a part-time customer service associate, I settled in to all the joyous perks of being paid to scan membership cards and fold towels with an upbeat demeanour and a sparkly grin: a free membership, minimum wage, and exclusively weekend shifts. Ah, the teenage years. But, it meant free access to all the fitness programs. And in this setting, with my newly acquired years of wisdom and fitness confidence (#sarcasm), I decided I was older, fitter and much better equipped to handle another one of these crazy "yoga" classes.

So I went.

And I was very confused.

This was not what I was expecting. It was not hard.

It felt too easy. It felt like I wasn't even getting a workout at all. It felt like I had wasted an hour of my time that I could have used to run myself into oblivion on the treadmill and burn at *least* 600 more calories in the same amount of time.

I spent all my time trying to make the sequences harder, because otherwise, what's the point? I was only concerned with attempting to do the highest possible option presented, even if my form was brutally sacrificed. I also spent a lot of the class trying to look at myself in the mirror once I'd gotten into whatever posture we were working towards. I rushed myself into the pose, and then checking out my reflection to see if I'd gotten it "right" in comparison to the instructor. I felt accomplished only when the former and the latter aligned accordingly.

I would also take note of the reflection of my body in all the varied twisted positions, to see if my belly looked fat or if my butt was protruding. I am seriously rolling my eyes right now.

I found a class that I enjoyed, with an instructor I really liked, but I only went once in a while, and I treated it like a "stretch" and a "freebie", that wasn't actually "getting me" anywhere. I treated yoga *only* as a workout.

Then one day, after a class that I had tried particularly hard at (but *still* wasn't able to get that *one* move at the highest option, and was noticeably frustrated about it), the sweet, gentle, and incredibly wise instructor came over, put a hand softly on my shoulder, and gave me an important and caring piece of advice. She said something like: "You'll know you're truly benefiting from the practice of Yoga when you can get through the entire class, and you do not notice anybody else in the room, or care about what your body looks like. And remember, Yoga is a practice, and is not meant to be *perfect*." (I'm paraphrasing, but if you're reading, that wisdom nugget was from you circa 2008-ish, Dawn! *Waves*)

This is (at an extremely tip-of-the-iceberg level, of course) what I would explain as: the wisdom of yoga. I had terrible misconceptions about yoga as a modality because of my first experience mistaking it for Pilates. I thought it was supposed to be "hard" and "demanding," and my perspective on fitness in general up to this point was that if it wasn't physical torture on my body, it most certainly wasn't a workout and thus, was not worth my valuable time. The opposite could not be truer, and it's pretty funny when I reflect back on the fact that I thought it was such an "invaluable waste of time" back then, when I had so many more hours at my leisure than I do now. When I first tried yoga, I was about 16 years old, single, and didn't have a child. Now I am 32, married, and have a four year old, and, yet, I make specific, important, scheduled time for yoga as if there isn't any other possible alternative. I make it a priority despite having even less time in my life to do it.

I wasn't able to truly appreciate the practice of yoga until I could learn to let go of the perfectionism, keep my eyes on my mat, and feel the benefits of a consistent practice reach outside the studio and into the rest of my life.

So, my advice is to think less about yoga being physical, and more about it being mindful. As someone with a bit of an addictive personality, along the way as I discovered more about yoga, I would gain momentum with my practice, and then have ridiculous expectations that I needed to go 6 times per week and keep that up on a regular basis. I once went on a crazy "hot yoga" binge myself, and did a hot yoga class every day for two weeks. It was MADNESS. And unnecessary. And then I didn't go again for several years. Do not set yourself such unrealistic expectations, please!

First of all, yoga can be done anywhere. You can find yoga videos on YouTube and on many online platforms any time you want! I even have quick and easy-to-follow yoga and meditation videos inside my online fitness program. Once you feel comfortable enough with the poses, you can just freestyle your own yoga. There's no right or wrong. Just find what feels good for your body, and move. Breathe. Flow.

Of course, further to the benefits of the Asanas,

or "poses" in yoga, is the benefit of acquiring valuable wisdom, knowledge, and perspective from your trained instructor. And THAT'S the good stuff, friends. It's a chance to get away from the stresses of life and motherhood, and spend an hour (or more!) focusing *only* on you. It's a chance to be mindful, to create intentional space for relaxation, to learn the value of focused breathing for balancing your body in a multitude of ways, and to experience the joy of passionate mindfulness that you can carry into the rest of your life to help you cope with the stress of everything else you encounter in your everyday life (poop-splosions at Walmart with no spare diapers included).

#MOMFIDENTAF

"If you start to decide that you don't fit into the standards you think are in place, you begin to question your own worth."

Chapter Twelve
BODY IMAGE AND STUFF

One of the biggest tools you can activate in order to be more at peace with your as-is mom-bod is awareness. If you can become aware of the things that trigger you into thinking you're anything less than a glorious, child-rearing, magnificent, worthy, and valuable gift to this human earth, you can begin the process of editing those things so they no longer have so much power. The way you see yourself and your worth and how you determine if you're "good enough" against the ridiculous societal standards we live in today is carefully crafted through a collective and ongoing picture of how you see yourself through your own eyes. How you measure up, if you fit in, and if you stand out. If you start to decide that you *don't* fit into the standards you think are in place, you begin to question your worth. Bit by bit, day after day, it doesn't happen overnight but eventually, after years of seeing "what's acceptable" against your reality, you get knocked down. Again and again.

Hopefully, with the help of my whispering ear (and a somewhat annoying but useful Chumbawumba song) you'll get back up again. Let's dig into body image and some tools for starting to paint a new picture, shall we?

Body image is your subjective picture or mental projection of your own body, and often we create a distorted picture based on what we see represented around us, what others have told us, what we see in magazines, and what is deemed "ideal" at the time. Usually, the "ideal" is something highly unattainable for the average woman, but yet splattered all over advertising as a way to sell products and prey on women's insecurities. Ever walked into Victoria's Secret, saw a great bra on one of those gorgeous models you see on the walls, taken one into the change room and had a little silent-cry where you may or may not have backed up against the wall and slid slowly to the floor dramatically like you were the climax in a scene from of *Full House*? (No? Just me?)

There are a lot of contributing factors to your overall body image, and I've already discussed how they may have come about from moments in your life where people around you moulded your impressionable mind with harmful comments, whether intentional or not. But we're also highly susceptible to advertising and marketing images that we have seen since we were kids, whether you noticed it or not. It may have burrowed its way in there subconsciously, but it's there.

Advertising is not very body inclusive. In fact, it's pretty body *ex*clusive and ridiculously specific. And when a company is trying to get you to buy something, they use people in their ads in a very strategic way. They want you to think that if you buy their product, your circumstances will emulate the ones you see in the image. Want to look like a Victoria's Secret model? Buy a Victoria's Secret bra! Want to have beautiful, smooth, perfect skin? Buy the cellulite cream in this magazine ad! Want to look as beautiful as the woman in that toothpaste commercial? Buy this toothpaste!

Advertising sells you more on an image, than on the actual product. Celebrities endorse products for this very same reason. Want to be as beautiful as Jennifer Aniston? Get yourself some Aveeno products and chug a bottle of Smart Water. That should do it! Marketing and advertising work in very strategic and orchestrated ways. We aren't able to change the fact that marketing exists and will always exist, probably with unrealistic portrayals of non-marginalized bodies and thin, white, beautiful, symmetrical, photoshopped people, but we can become damn clear about how we absorb these subliminal images. Do me a favour, would ya? Try a quick Google search for "McDonald's Commercial." See anything other than thin, apparently happy, beautiful people? Yet, McDonald's is not what I would call a very healthy choice. Even though they have slightly healthier options now than they have in the past, a burger and fries is their bread and butter, and as such, is typically what they're advertising. A thin, beautiful person taking down a burger. Sounds about right. They sell us on their food based on the people in their campaigns looking good and happy and thin and fit, and having a great time with their friends, and then we connect those generic models and their portrayed experience to the fact that they're eating the golden arches. I guess they also sell us on the fact that their food is not nutritious but highly satiating, because we crave salt and fat and sugar and their food is chocked full of all those things, which is also addictive. (For the record, I'm not against having McDonald's once in a while, because it's not going to fricken kill you. McDonald's is one of those "sometimes" foods; not super nutrient dense, so eating it every day isn't ideal. But you are not a bad person if you had McDonald's yesterday, or last Sunday morning after you partied hard at your BFF's wedding kid-free and woke up with a *smidge* of a hangover. No judgement. That was me last weekend.)

Sorry to throw McD's under fire, but it's a good example of how distorted our view can be of the products and services that are regularly marketed to us. Companies use beautiful, thin, generic people as avatars in their marketing so that you'll see the beautiful thin person and equate the product with being beautiful and thin. Then (they're hoping), you'll buy it. Ever taken a ~~photograph~~ screenshot to your hairdresser and said "I want my hair to look like [INSERT CELEBRITY]!" only to be thoroughly disappointed that you hop out of the salon chair but don't magically look exactly the same as Jessica Alba? (*DAMN!*) We are conditioned to want to look like, be like, act like everybody that we see in the media. It's why celebrities are paid millions for endorsements. It's why you feel your body isn't good enough because it doesn't look exactly like Jlo's. It's why we feel pressure to buy Spanx, and push-up bras, and to die our hair, and to constantly be searching for a quick fix that promises weight loss, because *in case you didn't know*, apparently happiness lies on the other side of those twenty pounds!

(I hope you can sense my sarcasm.)

We are a product of what we see. And we constantly see advertisements selling products telling us to look a certain way. Be smaller, lose weight, get skinny, detox, shred, get thin, have a bikini body, and get "summer-ready". So, of course, we think we need to do/be/have all those things. It's not your fault. It is, however, your responsibility to become more literate in this area if you want to build yourself up and feel good no matter what.

The next time you're out, in a public place, with heaps of people around you, I want you to complete this tiny tidbit of homework. Take a quiet, unbiased and judgement-free assessment of the humans around you. Who do they look more like? You? Or Beyonce? What percentage of people looks like that avatar most commonly used in print and commercial marketing? What percentage of people looks like your current avatar?

(Hopefully, the next public place you're at isn't a casting call for a Victoria's Secret runway show, or this theory may have blown up in my face.)

Seriously, though, if you can't remember to do this later, just think about this now: the last time you were at the mall, what kind of human bodies did you see? This is not an invitation to judge anyone's body, I simply want you to make the connection that there are FAR MORE people with average, normal, mid-sized bodies JUST LIKE YOURS than there are people who have perfect bodies. Did you know the average North American woman is a size fourteen, and the average "plus size model" wears a size eight? How distorting is that? We're all wandering around, thinking we aren't measuring up, when in reality we're the real women making up the statistical data, yet being made to feel like we're not normal for being "plus size." And then "plus size" isn't even accurately represented in advertising! It's a bit of a crock, if you ask me. It's a big issue to unpack and there's so much work to be done to re-construct the general image of female bodies, accurate representation, and diverse bodies in the media. But, girl, even that woman who appears to have a seemingly perfect body is often harsh and critical and judgemental of herself for some other silly reason, so if we let ourselves be heavily influenced by the things we see in the media IT'S A LOSE-LOSE SITUATION. Trust me, I've worked with women of all different shapes and sizes, and if it isn't a weight issue she's concerned about, it's *literally anything else*, because this bullshit affects us all to our cores.

I recently had someone approach me on Instagram and ask me how I can possibly lack confidence because I am [their words, verbatim] "clearly a good-looking, attractive woman who has a 'great body'". How can [I] be insecure when [I am] "attractive"? (Sidebar: While I have made massive strides in my own confidence game over the past several years, I often share my struggles with my community, and sometimes they're current issues. Yes, that's right, I still have days where I lack confidence, have low self-esteem, or exist in a spiral of negative self-talk that seems like it will never end. I am human, as are you. Nobody is immune from ever having bad days; nobody wakes up one day and never feels insecure or lacks confidence again. It's about *learning how to deal* with the bad days when the going gets tough. It's about turning a bad moment into a full-stop and re-directing instead of melting down and having that change room moment turn into a bad day, week, or month. We all struggle and that's what connects us. We're all in this together, babe.)

Well, I didn't know it when I responded to the message initially, but I found out later that this person was a man, a rare breed when it comes to my audience on social media.

Ahh. This makes sense. Please continue.

Men typically do not understand why we have such insecurity issues. At least the men I speak to. They just don't get why we're on the struggle bus in so many areas and for so many years of our lives; why we're so critical and judgemental of every single trait we have (or don't have.) There are many studies that show the comparison of confidence between men and women, and especially in our early 20s and 30s, men are far more confident than women in general. They also don't seem to talk about their insecurities in the way that women do. Ever sat around in a group of your besties and complained about shit you don't like about yourself? I know I have. And then what happens? Your friends probably negate whatever you've said, tell you something nice/kind/positive, and then they go on to say, "But MY legs though, well, they sure do suck the big one." So now you've learned that complaining about something will likely yield a short-term positive reinforcement from a friend, and that when someone else complains about their circumstances, you follow the exact same strategy and respond to their complaint with something positive. And the cycle repeats: complain about yourself, and get some type of external gratification from a friend. I would like to submit a hypothesis that comparatively, men DO NOT spend their valuable hangout time openly complaining about their weight gain, how they don't like their big arms, that their shoulders are too hairy, or that their penis is too small. I'm not saying they don't have insecurities, I think they do for sure. Some more than others. I think it dictates their behaviours more than we know and that ego drives a lot of their decisions when it comes to doing something with (or without) confidence. But they sure as shit don't sit around self-loathing in a group sharing circle with four bottles of "skinny-grape" wine and a bowl of low-calorie popcorn. Unless you know something I don't...

While we're here, I also recognize that *if* my hypothesis is in fact correct, and *if* men do not participate in self-loathing vent sessions like women do, it's probably due to their own gender-specific conditioning; the conditioning that tells boys and men not to open up about their feelings; the conditioning that insists they just "be a man" or "man up" and thus, be strong and avoid showing their emotions; and the conditioning that shouts for them to hold back any of those visible signs of emotion (except anger and rage asserting dominance, of course), and quit complaining. Men have their own bullshit life influences to deal with, I know. But, unfortunately, I am speaking from my own experiences in this book and I just don't have enough real-life experience to share my thoughts on why men don't body shame themselves as much as women. Maybe they do; maybe they just do it away from women. I want to be clear that I realize men also experience marketing and media pressures to have a specific body type; men also experience their own personal struggles with feeling confident; and men also struggle with appearance and representation in the media. So please don't write me an angry email about how I didn't include men or boys in this conversation, because that's not who I'm speaking to right now. And I recognize that they, too, have their own struggles when it comes to confidence, that's just not my demo, okay Karen-on-behalf-of-Karen's-husband? Thanks in advance, I appreciate it.

According to *Forbes*, women, on the other hand, seem to increase their confidence levels over time with age and experience and wisdom (I concur), while men stay about the same on an even keel[7]. I think that's because we just realize with age that snagging the cutest boy in school and coasting by on your *fingers crossed* good-looks is simply not as important in life compared to *allllll* the other cool shit we get to be a part of in this life. But in your early 20s, looking good is of exceptionally high priority, and caring what other people think about what you look like (see also: snagging cute boys) is basically your only goal in life outside passing that brutal college-prep math class.

But this particular question caught me off guard. It made me realize that how others see you is far different than how we see ourselves, and as I mentioned previously, other people are usually way less critical, despite what we may *think* they're thinking. And usually, they're not even thinking *anything* about us because they're too busy thinking about themselves. I think this is yet another fine realization we only come to with age and experience.

There sure is a lot of thinking going on here.

Think about the last time you were at the gym. Maybe you were wearing tight pants in a questionable colour. Maybe certain unmentionable areas of your body were sweating profusely and there was a very good chance there were sweat stains in more areas

---

[7] https://www.forbes.com/sites/jackzenger/2018/04/08/the-confidence-gap-in-men-and-women-why-it-matters-and-how-to-overcome-it/#35fe6bd73bfa

than just your pits. Maybe you were not sure what you were doing and meandered awkwardly through the weight equipment for twenty minutes before slipping onto a safe treadmill and catching up on your IG scroll. How much of your time was spent looking around and paying attention to every other person in there, analyzing what they were doing, wearing, saying; how they were moving or if they were doing things properly or sweating in interesting places?

My guess: little to none.

Why? Because we've already established that most of your available brain energy was spent thinking about *yourself*, and whether or not that guy over there noticed your hair hasn't been washed in 4 days. (He didn't. I couldn't be more positive of that.)

Everybody is thinking about their own personal #1 life priority: **themselves.**

Did guy-over-there notice you had a smidge of a camel-toe in your stone purple Lululemons? I mean... maybe. He *is* a guy. And he probably liked it, let's be real.

But did he spend more than a millisecond of time caring about it?

NEWP.

We spend far too much time thinking other people are thinking all these things about us, but they aren't.

I guarantee it. Because they're thinking about themselves. And if your answer to my earlier question was not, in fact, "little to none" and instead "an incredibly large amount of time", then my suggestion to you is to *STOP JUDGING THE FUCK OUT OF PEOPLE and you'll stop being so concerned that other people are judging you, Becky!* **Most** people are not paying attention. If you are paying attention like it's your job, then your inherent concern that others are judging you is because <u>that's what you are doing to others</u>. Does that make sense? You are constantly doing the behaviour, so you're assuming others are doing it to you. If you just realized you've been playing the role of judgey-mc-judgerson all this time and maybe you need a quality rehabilitation program, pronto - please stop reading now and find Gabrielle Bernstein's "Judgement Detox" on Amazon immediately. Click "buy with 1 click" and then come back here and finish. I'll wait here. *Checks watch*

Another quick example of people thinking about themselves the most: ever noticed someone relatively influential whom you follow on Instagram show up one day and apologize profusely for "being MIA for a bit"? And you're like, huh? I didn't even notice. #LOL. NOBODY NOTICED, JENNY. Oh, you're back? COOL! Didn't notice you were gone anywhere, but thanks for showing up again, I enjoy your antics and will continue watching.

As is life. Nobody else is paying *nearly* as much attention to you as you think they are. They're too busy worrying that you might be thinking something about them. Trust. It's a vicious self-centred cycle. Not in a bad way, I just want you to know that you can commence immediately the process of un-caring about what other people *might* think, because I can almost guarantee that 0.2% of people *actually* pay attention to what you're doing. And spending your valuable energy worrying about something you will *literally never, ever get the chance to actually confirm* anyway is a complete and utter useless waste of time.

Agreed? Great, then we can move on.

#MOMFIDENTAF

"Nobody else is paying nearly as much attention to you as you think they are. They're too busy worrying that you might be thinking something about them. Trust."

Chapter Thirteen

TAMAGOTCHIS, DIVERSITY, CONFORMITY AND CONFIDENCE

Think back to when you were in elementary school. Think about the earliest time you remembered there being a "trend" that you really wanted to participate in. Everybody was doing it, and you wanted IN so you could be one of the "cool kids". This will of course depend largely on the generation and culture you grew up in (most prevalent in Western/North American society) and what socioeconomic and personal circumstances you experienced, but I think it translates to most of us going through the school system.

The earliest "trend" I remember attempting *hard* to participate in was owning a Tamagotchi when I was in grade 4. Everybody had one. They all wore them around their necks on bathtub-chain necklaces and played with them at every possible moment. I wanted one. I neeeeeeded one. I begged my mom for one. And I think I had to wait until my birthday to get one (well done, parents!) But when I did get one, it was so gratifying to *fiiiinally* be able to participate in the trend and feel like I "belonged" with everybody else, like I fit in, like I connected with those who were participating in the trend too, and like I understood everybody else and they understood me.

If we really break this down, I can see how this example actually slips easily into the "psychological needs" component of Maslow's (classic) Hierarchy of Needs[8]. Quick overview/refresher, since you probably learned about this at some point in high school: Humans need things like food, water, warmth, safety and security *first*, but next on the pyramid of things we crave is "belongingness and love", like intimate relationships and friendships, and "esteem needs" like prestige and feeling of accomplishment.

Getting the "thing" everybody else had equated naturally to—feeling a part of something; feeling understood and accepted by others; creating a connection with other humans based on shared experience and thus sharing common ground and interest for conversation... which all felt good and probably

8 https://www.psychologytoday.com/ca/blog/hide-and-seek/201205/our-hierarchy-needs

prompted the secretion of those feel-good hormones like serotonin and dopamine - which is addictive and warrants us looking for another "hit", even in the fourth grade.

The Tamagotchi example may or may not resonate with you, but I'm sure you have your own story of remembering a certain product, piece of clothing, footwear, makeup, hairstyle or other aesthetic trend that you felt pressure to participate in so that you "fit in" as a susceptible, easily influenced pre-teen. It's bold and hard and unpopular to go against the grain when you're young, vulnerable, and still finding yourself as a person. Also, kids are fucking *mean*. The moment you don't do something that everybody expects you'll do; the moment you dare to be brave and speak up, disagree, and don't do what everybody else is doing, it makes other young, susceptible, insecure kids uncomfortable. And the natural reaction to that? Poking fun at the behaviour. Deflection from them being uncomfortable, to making YOU feel uncomfortable.

In case you're wondering, unfortunately these behaviours don't always just go away after you're done school, folks. Nope. Adults continue to participate in this behaviour, too. Doing something outside the norm? People will look. Stare, even. With perplexed facial expressions they don't know how to politely hide. Some people will make comments. If you couple your "outside the norm" behaviour with sharing vulnerably about it on Facebook, you're bound to get some annoying, self-centred, ego-driven comments peppered with questionable emojis. You might even get someone passive aggressively sharing their seemingly "helpful" opinion ("Oh, wow! Good for you. I would, like, NEVER do that personally, but like, to each her own!"). They're pretending to be supportive but actually they're just being condescending. So is there a solution here? No. Not really. Sorry! My advice is: just do whatever you want and be prepared that not everybody will understand. Like if you're still carrying around a Tamagotchi today. Some people may think that's odd and want to make comments. I say: YOU DO YOU, GIRL. Sarah from high school does not need to understand what you're up to, and she is entitled to whatever facial expression or comment she wants, at the end of the day. You cannot control what other people do, or how they react to you. You can only control YOU. Your actions, your re-actions. You. Do. You.[9]

The experiences we carry from elementary/high/post-secondary school to our adult life often reinforces that age-old assumption that we should work really

---

[9] There's actually a really great book by this title that I would highly recommend. *You Do You* is by one of my favourite authors and you will not regret reading any of the works in her "No F*cks Given" series of books! Sarah Knight – *You Do You - How to be Who You Are and Use What You've Got to Get What You Want* - http://nofucksgivenguides.com/ydy/

hard to "fit in" and do what everybody else is doing, wear what everybody else is wearing, make our bodies look the way they're "supposed to" look, and think what everybody else is thinking, so others don't notice us and/or as a result, make fun of us, because that doesn't feel good. We know this. We may not even be able to explain the feeling, but we know the consequences for breaking conformity. And if you think back to when this first showed up for you, is it definitely not something any kid *wants* to face for the rest of their adolescence, so we learn behaviours to combat it. We strive to fit in at all costs. We are willing to do whatever it takes to accomplish fitting in, slip under the radar, and not be the focus for some bully to highlight for the rest of the group. And that behaviour becomes our conditioning. We repeat it over and over, even into our lives as grown-ass women who are, in case you didn't know FULLY able to do whatever the fuck we want with ourselves, our lives, our bodies, our relationships, our parenting, our jobs... everything.

The pressure to conform is real. I remember being pressured to try alcohol, to smoke, to talk to or kiss boys, to listen to very specific music, to buy a particular brand of makeup, shoes, clothing; to shoplift (I didn't BTW! I promise, Mom!), to behave a certain way, to believe certain things, to cut and colour my hair... among 17 billion other things. One time in 1993 I really and truly wanted the new Spice Girls CD but was instead influenced by my cool friend to get *Pieces of You* by Jewel. I regretted that decision immediately after listening to "Who will Save your Soul" three times and realizing I didn't like any of the other songs. I realize this wildly informative overview of my teenage-dom doesn't directly help you get over your own personal insecurities, but I'm getting there, I promise. The point is, your friends in real life may not be currently pressuring you to pick up a pack of cigs and light 'em up, but the people you hang out with, the places and things your eyes see every day as you move through life, and *especially* marketing, advertising and social media (that's impossible not to notice these days) - are all contributing to the likelihood of you feeling pressure to look and act a certain way. To "fit in" and be socially accepted, even as a grown-ass woman.

This pressure can trickle in from all kinds of sources and maybe you don't even realize where some of your behaviours or consumer buying decisions have been impacted. Let me ask you this: do you have any makeup or beauty products in your bathroom cupboards? How many, would you say? Are there any products to make your hair smoother or silkier? Are there any skin-related products that help "smooth fine lines and wrinkles" and/or adjust the tone and shade of your natural skin? Are there any products related to diminishing cellulite or the appearance of stretch marks and scars? Are there any traditional makeup products, like eyeshadow palettes, lipstick, eyeliner and mascara? How many hair products do you own? Do you have hair appliances that adjust the natural texture of your hair?

You've purchased all of these things based on the pressure to conform to what you think you "should" look like. Right? And that image has been curated and influenced by all the things you see on a regular basis, whether you notice it or not. Our goal now will be to practice awareness moving forward. Let's think about what you actually require for the maintenance of good hygiene and overall health, shall we? A toothbrush and toothpaste? A hairbrush maybe? Some type of deodorant? A bar of soap and some shampoo? Maybe nail clippers, and if we're really getting boujee, some type of body lotion to keep your skin hydrated? Putting 30 products in your hair, slathering your skin, eyes, and mouth with 79 artificial makeup products, and wearing tummy-control underwear beneath your office wear is not due to your basic hygiene requirements. It's based on what you think you need to look like and what's accepted in the culture and society you live in.

Sidebar: I'd like to add that my intention for explaining the contrast between "basic hygiene needs" and "what you have purchased as a consumer" is not (like, ever) to throw shade at you for wearing makeup, colouring your hair, or applying a cream that promises to make your skin firmer. I have a butt-load of commercial products in my bathroom, too. I wear makeup on a regular basis, too. I put products in my hair, straighten or curl it with an appliance, and try to dress myself in a flattering way, too. Because we are allowed to do what makes us feel the best and there's nothing wrong with wanting to up-level and enhance your au natural state, even though I want you to know that there is absolutely nothing wrong with your au natural state and the makeup and hair and clothing is not mandatory - but if it makes you feel good THAT'S FLIPPING AWESOME. So, no, this is isn't a call to go dump every product from your bathroom in the garbage because you're a terrible human for wanting to enhance your features. Just so we're clear on that. I do, however, encourage you to think critically about how and why you feel "less than" in the first place, if you don't enhance your natural features with makeup and other products. Is there something there you need to address? Do you need to do some unsexy personal work, even though you plan to continue wearing make-up? I never want you to hide and I most definitely want you to question how you feel about yourself, naked or not. Regular self-assessment is key to finding what feels good for you.

Do you feel like it would be acceptable to show up to work with hair that wasn't washed or styled, a "naked" face, and unkempt clothing? Actually, some places I'm sure this wouldn't be such a big deal, but there are many places that actually have a corporate policy for adhering to "personal grooming" standards, which sometimes even includes restrictions on having visible piercings outside your ear-holes, and visible tattoos in order to "look professional". Why? Because face piercings and visible tattoos are things society considers to be "outside the lines", and as we've already established, that whole system is designed to keep you inside the lines so you "fit in", where it's generally safer from ridicule and judgement.

Media, marketing and advertising also work explicitly for companies that promote products that try to get you to **buy them**, so that again, you fit into the ideal "look" that apparently, everybody is dying to be. This is why it's so important to pay attention to what you're looking at with a very critical eye. It takes time to get to that point, and to find a nice balanced state where you don't constantly think every company and person who sells a product is out to "target" or "get you", but it's definitely worth considering. We've touched on this briefly already, but it's worth reminding you again because the way we view things around us plays such a massive role on how we evaluate ourselves and our realities. If we compare ourselves with the false representation of perfection in most visual marketing, we create a skewed view. Clothing companies use thin, beautiful women to model and sell their clothing. Fitness brands use thin, beautiful people to sell the promise of what their service can do to your body. Food companies use thin, beautiful people to get you subconsciously connecting that image with their product so you'll buy it. Companies use social media and many thin, beautiful influencers and celebrities (who are, come on, pretty much always thin and beautiful) to sell their products through social influence. Television shows, movies, and commercials use thin, beautiful actor-people to star in their productions. Companies use thin, beautiful people in advertisements on the pages of magazines to get you to buy their products.

Because most of the world views "thin and beautiful" as the ultimate, highly coveted accomplishment that apparently everybody wants to strive for and be, thin, beautiful people are the ideal candidates to literally be EVERYWHERE, and whether you're buying those products or not, you are subconsciously seeing that thin, beautiful, often white people with "ideal body types" are the most represented and therefore the most sought after. And even if you didn't think you gave a shit about accomplishing the "ultimate goal" of being thin and beautiful, think about the circle you hang with (or hung with in high school or college) and if your conversations ever centred around diet or weight-loss themes. You could have grown up in a house where your own mother or other female influence was constantly dieting and trying to "be skinny", or you could have missed that (yay!) but then noticed all your friends were constantly striving to lose weight and look a certain way and openly picking themselves apart in front of a mirror like Regina George on a regular basis. Even if you're the Cady in this situation, eventually, social influence bites you a bit. Eventually, you notice that everybody's having a carrot stick and a diet Coke for lunch. Eventually, you notice that the girls who seem to have some genetically obtained privileges are getting all the attention and focus. It's no wonder a girl's confidence level and self-esteem generally piques at the age of fourteen[10]. This shit is real and rancid. (This is one of the reasons I created a girls-version of my best-selling *#MOMFIDENT AF Self-Love Journal*. Because girls should be working on this stuff before they get to be women and moms and have to de-condition themselves from years of perpetual self-esteem challenges. It's called "Yes I can, #WatchMe" and it's a confidence, self-love and gratitude journal for girls aged 7-14. Check it out on my website if you want some more information! GetMomfidentAF.com)

With a little help from your fabulous and complex brain comparing your reality to what you are seeing

---
10   https://www.nytimes.com/2018/10/01/well/family/confidence-gap-teen-girls-tips-parents.html

everywhere, it's way too easy to come to the conclusion that you do not look just like that thin, beautiful representation you see everywhere, and therefore deduce that you are *not good enough*. I will add that there are a few companies who are starting to get it right, and who are now including more diverse body representation in their advertising campaigns and it is GLORIOUS. Canadian-based brand Knixwear, for example, uses real women who are customers of their brand in their marketing campaigns. Along with this being an essential move in the right direction, it is actually a smart marketing strategy in my opinion, and there's nothing wrong with that fact. I am gladly an ideal customer of theirs and their advertisements make me feel seen and represented and that makes me want to support the company. That's just good business, because selling products is the ultimate goal of any company, and there's nothing wrong with that. But Knixwear speaks to me with their real women showing stretch marks and full figures among long and lean silhouettes, along with many other body types and ethnicities in-between, and I've purchased many products from them because I felt connected to the real bodies I saw in their marketing. So that's a job well done for Knixwear, and is so important if we want to start showing the world what real bodies look like. PSA: The bathing suit I'm wearing on the cover of this book is a Knixwear[11] bathing suit. I am a huge advocate for their brand.

I really don't know who came up with the idea that thin and beautiful is the only avatar that people will buy from, but I feel a lot more empowered to buy a product from a company who uses a model that looks more like ME, than I am to cross my fingers and hope that this bra makes me look like the "angel" that's modelling it. Know what I'm sayin'? This is also not a call for you to bash thin, beautiful people, guys. They are just as valuable and worthy, too. There are so many different types and sizes and versions of beauty in this world, and it's a shame that uniqueness and difference is not celebrated more. I hope we get there someday. I really just want thin body ideals to be there *alongside* other various versions of real bodies, so the women of the world can see that they are normal, included and accepted, too.

Oh, I guess I forgot to finish the story about how I handled my obscure male follower who actually took the time to send me a private message on Instagram to directly inquire about the validity of my apparently unwarranted insecurities. In a nutshell, I had to explain to this man (who was very respectful and nice, and actually not at all creepy or inappropriate given the circumstances, btw!) that... the thing is, unfortunately,

---

11 www.knixwear.com - seriously, check them out!

insecurity does not discriminate. I've yet to come across a woman who honestly and openly is 100% secure, confident, happy and self-assured *all* of the time. In my experience, even the woman who *looks like* she fits the "ideal" body and beauty standards that society throws at us, STILL has her own personal insecurities, though they may be different than yours or mine. Which is absolutely unfortunate, but very real. I wish it wasn't this way, but women are generally so susceptible to feeling pressure to conform, to fit in, to look the way they think they're "supposed" to look, based on the repetitive images we see every day in media representations, on TV, in advertisements, and on social media.

Men do not seem to be *as* susceptible as women are to conforming to that "perfect" ideal male body type, though I know there is some effect on them. Most think they need to have rock hard arms and chiseled pecs in order to attract the opposite sex. But it seems like that's typically the only thing a man is worried about - sex - (the opposite, and see also: having it) and so he isn't as concerned about a real woman looking exactly like a model in a magazine. And if we're talking about the prospect of you getting with a man (whether this is a potential love interest or your own boyfriend or husband, if you're heterosexual of course!) they're really far more interested in the fact that you *want* to get with him than anything else. Trust. Husbands and partners included. The most attractive things are always a) your confidence, and b) your desire to get jiggy. Seriously.

This is not rocket science, girls. This book is not about having sex, but for the purpose of this chapter, here's your homework: if you are in a relationship right now, put your confidence on tonight, and initiate intimacy with your partner in whatever way feels natural to you (and maybe a tiny smidge outside your comfort zone). Show your partner that you **want** to have sex. I can almost guarantee that your partner does not care if you lose 30 pounds, have a tummy roll, have visible stretch marks, cellulite or have a less than perfectly groomed nether-region. He (or she) just wants you to *want* to do it.

So this man was like, scratching his head as to why someone who appears to be attractive, by conventional standards I guess, who is healthy and of average size would ever be lacking confidence or having any insecurities. And it was a bit of a tricky concept to explain, because he really couldn't see how I would ever think of myself as "not good enough" or compare myself to anybody who wasn't me, because why should I compare? I am not anybody else but myself. This is not ground breaking information by any means, but it's worth the explicit reminder here, friends:

YOU ARE NOT ANYBODY ELSE BUT YOURSELF.

You are not going to look exactly like that model,

or actress, or influencer, and why should you? You are literally the only version of you both inside and out, and you have the ability to own your unique traits, build your personal strengths, acknowledge your weaknesses, enhance your features and rock the shit out of the body you have **right this very moment**, even if it you have the desire to make some type of external change. You are the only one responsible for building your confidence game. You are the only one responsible for figuring out how to practice self-acceptance. You are the only one who can manage and modify the thoughts cycling through your brain at any given moment. You are the one who must decide to put in the work in order to truly love and respect yourself and your body as you move forward in this crazy game of life.

What purpose does it serve you to live in an existence of constant hate and distaste for your body? What benefit do you gain from complaining to yourself or others; from shaming yourself in the dressing room for going up a size; for agonizing over your belly roll, stretch marks, scars, veins, thick thighs, broad shoulders, weight, size, shape or other feature that literally only contributes to one very small percentage of your entire being? Your body is your vessel, and you should learn how to take care of that thing so you can live a healthy, balanced life. But there is no rule that says your vessel needs to fit into a pre-determined box of specific traits. You may feel that way based on how susceptible we are to the representation we see on a regular basis, but there is no rule. You get to decide how to be confident, in a way that works for you. You get to decide what soundtrack plays inside your head. You get to decide how you respond to a comparison your brain makes, and how you evaluate yourself against something else that you see. You get to determine that you are worth so much more than just what the outside of your body looks like.

YOU ARE A VALUABLE AND COMPLEX HUMAN WHO DESERVES TO TAKE UP SPACE AND YOU ARE NOT DEFINED BY YOUR SIZE.

This may take some time to accept and the thought process will ruminate for a while before it lands, but your end-goal in life in order to be confident and happy does not need to be "obtain the correct level of skinny-ness" and then everything else will fall into place perfectly.

Thin and beautiful does not equal happy.

Thin and beautiful does not equal confident.

Thin and beautiful does not equal the solution to all of life's problems.

Thin and beautiful does not equal love.

Thin and beautiful does not equal success.

Thin and beautiful does not equal a good person.

Some people are naturally thin and beautiful. Some people work very hard to fit that one archetype and spend their lives agonizing over every decision that may keep them fitting the profile. Some people long to be smaller but don't know what they're doing "wrong." Some people have naturally big frames and will never achieve that "thin" body ideal. Some people give zero fucks whether they fit any specific profile or not, and go on to *gasp* live glorious lives full of love and acceptance and happiness and success and joy and being great, full-of-life people — regardless of their shape or size, big, small, tall, thin, thick, wide, or slim.

I want you to be one of those people. But, girl, you've gotta put in work.

"In a society that profits from your self-doubt, liking yourself is a rebellious act."
—Caroline Caldwel

#MOMFIDENTAF

"What purpose does it serve you to live in an existence of constant hate and distaste for your body? (Spoiler alert: None. Literally zero amount of purpose.)"

Chapter Fourteen

ANTI-SOCIAL MEDIA

Okay, okay. It's time we talk about the elephant in the book that I haven't talked a lot about yet. The elusive self-esteem-crushing tool that makes it easy to see Nana across the country and keep up with Laura from elementary school, but extremely difficult to keep your sanity and happiness with the constant opportunity to compare hanging in the balance. Well, friends, social media is here to stay. I'm pretty sure, anyway. The platforms may change, I don't know that Instagram will be king for much longer, but our lives have been forever changed with Mark Z's contribution to the world and I don't think there's any going back now. You probably have your own opinions about it, and I do, too. I have an ongoing love/hate relationship with the entire social media world, and I could probably write an entire book about this phenomenon alone, but instead you'll just get a Coles' notes style chapter. (Hooray for you!)

The platforms that have been designed to keep us connected and in touch with everyone and everything in our lives, are somehow assisting us with becoming the most disconnected, unsocial and unhappy bunch of comparison-centred people in history. Social platforms and the influx of technology available to us at any given moment have the potential to interfere with real social experiences and relationships, and they do. Often. We check in on Facebook or Instagram during the (normal!) lulls and silences in a real-life conversation. We update our status without actually ever speaking or saying the thought to another human, muttering it only in virtual form. We take photos and post them for everyone to see, as if the experience wasn't real or valid unless someone else double-taps, acknowledges it, or says "me too!"

If you want my honest opinion, I feel that social media has the potential to hurt us more than it has the potential to help us. Sometimes, I feel like throwing my phone in the ocean like Carrie Bradshaw in the first *Sex and the City* movie, and declaring that if anyone wants to know anything about me, they will need to find me and connect in person to know it. (Not before putting that as my Facebook status, of course... JK JK.)

I say this lightly, because of course I have an online business and brand that social media is a large part of. In fact, my business has grown almost completely due to the 'media' part of my social connections. I've sold out coaching programs, launched and sold hundreds of copies of my Self-Love Journals and other books, filled in-person workshops, and created real-life relationships that were initially sparked via a virtual connection. Heck, there's a good chance you came across the book in your hands right now because of social media. That's pretty cool! I've even made some of my closest friends and business colleagues by initially connecting online. So, of course there are benefits to being connected and building a community or business in the online space, as a marketing and networking tool.

However, social media, if we aren't careful, is going to be a detriment to the next generation. If you've ever finished scrolling your Insta and had those feelings of insecurity, "not-good-enough-ness", felt jealousy or inadequacy, felt like your skills are lacking, like you're missing out, or missing the mark, like you aren't a good enough mom, like someone else is doing things better than you, or if you've ever felt like your life just isn't as good as what you just saw while thumbing a glass screen... well, I'm here to tell you a few things.

First of all, and what will form the basis of the rest of this entire chapter, is this: social media *is what it is.*

It's of course designed to connect us to people, and that does happen lots of times. It helps us keep in touch with a friend who moved far away, whom you're still very much interested in knowing and seeing what they and their family and children are up to. It can help *your* mom or grandmother keep up to date with what you're doing from wherever you are. It has many cool, positive attributes. But what it's grown into is a space where everyone shares with you the very best pieces of their lives. Literally. Only the best. It is rare to find someone sharing the actual reality of their lives. The actual mess. The actual not-so-positive feelings that we all experience but that nobody talks about because, why share your discomfort with everybody? Nobody prefers to admit that they lost their job, are going through a divorce, or couldn't afford to go on vacation this year.

The best parts of life are captured. Not the uncomfortable, unhappy ones. Not the fights with your spouse, the spilt milk on the floor, the argument with your mom, the messy house, the loads of undone laundry, the email that said you didn't get the promotion… only the best parts are worth taking out a camera and snapping a memory. So there's that. Step one to accepting social media for what it is: know that it is pretty much a manipulated, "best of" version of life showcased only in its highest, most attractive state, and you should take it with a grain of salt, because life has many lows, too.

For every perfectly framed image of someone's recently decorated laundry room, there's piles of undone laundry behind the camera, kids toys, counters filled with shit that will eventually be crammed into the junk drawer when company comes over, and a kitchen sink filled with dishes that somehow haven't been put into the dishwasher yet, even though it's clean and empty.

Then, not only do we have only the "good stuff" to pull from, that one qualified image is often cropped, edited, filtered, angled preferably, and only then is it deemed good enough to be posted on the social platform for others to see. But this is kind of like, how you'd show up to a party, a friend's wedding, or even just to your day job, right? You don't show up in view of others in sweatpants, with bedhead and yesterday's makeup; you get it together, you make yourself presentable in whatever way works for you, and that's how the external world views "you." You dictate how they view you. You get to edit and choose what people see when you socialize. Only, that isn't the *real, raw* you, it's the one you've tidied up and have prepared to be a bit shinier, and there's nothing wrong with that. That's how social media is, for the most part. I understand why only the good stuff is shared. It isn't really socially acceptable to be openly blabbing away about all your downfalls IRL, as chances are, you want to talk about what's going right in your life, and that's great! Why wouldn't you? The difference is that this image of perfection has been massively multiplied and you're able to see about a thousand people's "best of" in a five minute thumb-scroll. That's a lot of perfection compared to your real circumstances, and that's tricky for your brain to process.

A follower asked me once about my opinion on the excessive use of photo filtering and body-altering apps used in conjuction with social media. I understand the inquiry; it's a confusing world we live in when most of the things we see are not 100% real, even the photos from the average people we see on a regular basis. In case you didn't know, everyone from Kylie Jenner to your local coffee-shop barista has the ability to easily edit and alter their photos for public posting with the same kind of techniques (and often, quality) as professional photoshopping programs. Your old bestie from high school could very well be taking the best photo she took out of eight thousand, and then popping it into FaceTune and squishing her waist and inflating her ta-tas so she looks, you know, "more proportionate". (According to *who*, exactly?) She can edit her skin so it has no pimples; whiten her teeth fourteen shades; make her nose look smaller; and even make her freaking eyeballs closer together, if she wants to. Then she can slap a filter on top of it to adjust the lighting and tone of the image. So, when I say that nothing is really "real" on social media, this is what I mean, and I don't think it's really *news* to anyone at this point. Overall, here's my opinion: we're never going to be able to stop people from filtering. The technology is there, and it's a real shame that so many women feel the need to make these adjustments before deeming their photos "acceptable", but I will never be able to control what other people do. I can only control what *I* do. And it doesn't serve me at all to sit around complaining that everybody else is virtually nipping, tucking, and filtering and how it's so very damaging to everybody else. It *is* damaging, absolutely, but no matter how much I preach about it, I'm never going to be able to stop everybody in the world from this behavior. Instead, I focus on the things I have control over. I can control my awareness of the issue, and I have decided to just call a spade a spade. *Not everything you see on social media is real.* Duh. People edit themselves. Period. If you go into the platform(s) knowing this, you will feel less like the wool has been pulled over your eyes. *It's. Mostly. Fake.* Accept it. Social media is like Twinkies. Twinkies are technically consumable food, but they're mostly fake. You might still eat them, even though you *know* they're full of garbage and literally nothing nutritious, but you have just made peace with the fake-ness. (I bet you've never compared Instagram to Twinkies before, have you? HA!) Go into social media knowing it's heavily false, or... don't use it? I don't know. Once I realized that everyone and their brother could use photoshopping apps to adjust themselves, I just decided to take social media for what it is. Being pissed that everybody be filterin' does not solve any problems. I am at peace with the fact that a photo sharing app includes 90% edited content, and it's out of my control what other people do, anyway.

Where was I? Oh yeah. So, we have the good parts of our lives, carefully edited and filtered, posted on our "wall" for everyone to see. And then, as if that's not enough, we are secretly hoping that once we post it, we'll get some external validation from someone, *anyone*, that confirms, yes, thank goodness, they "like" what we're doing, too. And when we get those "likes" that support or agree with us? When we get that validation from external sources? It's just like the feeling of fitting in back in elementary school. It gives us a hit of happy hormones and we crave it again and again. Well, shit. The complexities of social media and its impending influence on self-worth and self-esteem are far more damaging to the younger generation than they are to us, as grown-ass women, but it can definitely still manifest as negative comparison energy even as an adult. Kids and teens do not have fully developed brains or impulse control function at their age, and so the connections to social apps and their ability to cause harm is far greater for our kids. Which is why I'm a little terrified about my four-year-old becoming a fourteen-year-old. Fuck, it's probably more like "becoming a seven-year-old" with the way things have been going lately. But that doesn't mean you haven't been affected in some way, even subconsciously, by the themes of inadequacy that social media can perpetuate.

Okay, so, that's all well and good. We know that people post the highlight reel. The filtered highlight reel. I'm not the first person to notice this, I'm sure you've heard and seen that before. Noted. The part that eludes us is the comparison to everyone else's personal reel. We don't compare on purpose. Sometimes we even remind ourselves about the old highlight-reel effect, and continue on with our day. But over days, weeks, months…years of seeing this type of content over and over, mindlessly scrolling, subconsciously we start wondering why "not good" stuff happens in our own lives. Then, we compare the not-good stuff to all the good stuff we see all the time, and over time, with consistency and repetition, this ultimately has the potential to harm your self-worth, your self-image, your body image, your confidence, your mindset and mental health, because you're evaluating your own personal circumstances against someone else's fake (or, at least dramatically filtered) ones. Allow me to give you some examples of what your internal dialogue may be whispering to you:

Why aren't I as successful as Karen? She gets every job she goes for.

Why aren't I as good of a mom as Jennifer? She never says anything bad about her kids.

Why aren't I as fit as Carol? She is in great shape and is motivated to workout every day.

Why don't I have an Apple watch like Julia? She has an iPad too. She has everything she wants. Why don't I?

Why isn't my house as clean as Sarah's? Everything is always in its place and perfectly polished.

Why don't I eat as well as Becky? She must have all day to make beautiful, healthy, organic and vegan meals all day.

Why isn't my marriage as good as Gina's? She is so connected to her partner and they go on all kinds of nice trips.

It would be totally normal to feel some of this comparison or even jealousy in your life, if you were hearing about all the same things socially in your small circle, like women used to back in the day. But if you were really and truly close to any of those people (like women were back then, at least more often) you'd probably also know that Karen had lost three different roles before landing the Director position. But she isn't going to post about that.

You'd know that Jennifer is struggling to manage a three-nager and had a public crying meltdown in the grocery store yesterday while both kids screamed bloody murder in the cart. You'd know that Carol has a severe eating disorder fueled by a toxic relationship with her boyfriend, who forces her to workout every day even when she doesn't want to. You'd know that Julie has an Apple watch and an iPad that were gifted to her from her parents instead of them visiting for her birthday, and she'd happily trade time with her parents in lieu of expensive shit. You'd know that Sarah has a housekeeper and that when you come to visit in person, her house is not as picture perfect as it is on Instagram. You'd be able to see that, yes, Gina and her husband travel and have a great relationship, but they go to therapy once a week and travelling is part of their commitment to maintaining all the hard work they put in to make their relationship work, because they almost got divorced last year. You'd know a mixture of both good and bad things about all of these women, and so then you'd be able to see yourself in their stories. You'd be able to see the whole story, not just the good part of the story. You'd know the shitty stuff and the brilliant stuff. So when you saw the good stuff, you'd know that there are ebbs and flows and that your own personal ebbs and flows are totally normal.

Social media has the power to make us think our

ebbs are not natural. Our bad experiences and moods, negative feelings, arguments, difficult times, lost jobs, fertility issues, and horrible days are unusual, because everything we see is picture perfect.

And so what I am going to reiterate again is this: social media *is what it is*, and the good news is, you have a conscious choice *always* to a) be aware of what you're seeing and know that it isn't all real stuff, all the time and b) unfollow the crap out of people who make you feel anything but happy! It's a perfectly curated highlight of people's lives. It's often a snapshot of all the pretty, positive things and not the ugly, negative things. It's the visual equivalent of bumping into an acquaintance and mustering up your dreaded small-talk muscles to tell her everything's "Great! You know, just really busy! We should have coffee soon!" Instead of sharing openly that you just lost a parent and you hate your job and you're experiencing anxiety and having a really fucking hard time at life right now. We don't do that in person, and people don't do that on social media, either. Vulnerability connects us and is an incredible tool for humans. If you truly know a person, you know their life is not picture perfect all the time. There are good parts, and hard parts. But generally, we don't open with vulnerable.

So when you feel yourself comparing or questioning, remember that there is way more to the story than just what you see on social media (or what you hear when you chat with Janet in the school drop-off line). The squares you see on Instagram, the status updates and photos you see on Facebook... those are the things the person wants you to see. We are allowed to control what goes out there, so why would we share unflattering photos of bad times in our lives? Why would we take a selfie of our mascara-stained face after a big fight with our partner? Why would we post our "progress pics" on #TransformationTuesday of us gaining weight? Everybody wants to put their best self forward. In the same way you wouldn't show up to a friend's engagement party in your husband's stained university sweatpants, no make-up and unwashed hair, you aren't going to post the most unflattering version of your life for the world to see, either. Right?

We all post the best version, and there isn't necessarily anything wrong with that. If you're reading this and you have social media, I want you to consider what you typically post out there. Unflattering photos of yourself? A picture of your kid having a meltdown at Target? A kitchen sink full of dishes? A selfie of you after having a fight with your best friend? I'd venture a guess the answer is no to all of those. We are all craving recognition and acceptance, and we all long to control and contribute to the best-looking version of ourselves, online or in person. Even if behind the curtain, you're having a really rough go at life, you probably show up online as a better version of that, so outsiders don't know what's really going on. But it's easy to forget that when you're looking at what everybody else is doing, and it doesn't mirror your reality that's full of flaws and hard times and challenges and shitty days, mixed in with the good stuff.

So my advice is, again, to just **take social media for what it is.** Perfect versions of everything. Don't let it get to you. Take breaks from it. Follow people who give you good feelings. There is a behind the scenes to every photo and story you're seeing. Go into it knowing that and you can shift your expectation drastically. At the end of the day, I can guarantee you that nobody's life is perfect. The grass is always greener. The person who is posting the thing you're comparing yourself to probably wants something you have, or what someone else has. They have their own issues, their own difficulties, unique to them, but unless you get to know them personally, you're never going to know about them. Accept that, and you should be better equipped to handle the social media game.

#MOMFIDENTAF

"There's nothing worse than complaining but not taking action to move towards something better, even just a little bit better."

Chapter Fifteen
MAKING MOM-NECTIONS

I heard at a conference in 2018 while listening intently to one powerhouse of a happiness doctor and a good friend of mine, Dr. Gillian Mandich[12], that the single most important contributing factor to a person's happiness is social interaction. Not social connection online, but actual *interaction* and *connection* with humans in real life. I don't know about you, but whenever I've spent some time with a friend or family member, without an agenda, without a specific purpose, but just spending that time engaging and connecting... I always feel better afterwards. Even if that wasn't the intention or purpose of the hangout sesh. Somehow life's struggles and challenges don't seem as bad. Somehow the person you're

---

[12] http://www.gillianmandich.com/

connecting with helps you to feel more valuable and worthy, simply by sharing their valuable and precious time and energy with you. Somehow you're able to feel heard and valued and listened to, and to hear what someone else is going through and connect on a level of understanding much deeper than the surface.

Social connection is truly where it's at. I think there's a resurgence of workshops and in-person events for good reason. People want to feel connection, whether they know the reason for it or not. We are hard-wired for *real* connections as humans, and even though we're technically the most "connected" society of people in history, we're desperately craving human interaction and if we don't work hard at it, we will not get what we intrinsically crave. In a *Psychology Today* article titled "Connect to Thrive", PT reports that a "lack of social connection is a greater detriment to health than obesity, smoking and high blood pressure. On the flip side, strong social connection leads to a 50% increased chance of longevity."[13] So, there. I'm not making this stuff up, pal. We literally come out of the womb and are immediately placed on another human's chest because skin-to-skin is scientifically proven to improve the health of the baby. There's a reason intimacy includes mental connection but also actual physical skin-to-skin connection. Humans literally *need*

---

13   https://www.psychologytoday.com/ca/blog/feeling-it/201208/connect-thrive

this shit. It's in our DNA. And we're currently deflecting a lot of it because of technology. This is a real problem.

Sure, it's easy and convenient to hang out on FaceTime, or send someone a text, or say hi over Instagram; and it's more difficult, time consuming and logistically challenging to create space to actually *be* with someone, and how you feel about connecting with people will also be widely different depending on your personality type. However, it's so crucial to actually make time for this in your schedule, just like you're penning in a dentist appointment or a yoga class. I get it, if you're in introvert, you may struggle with the thought of hanging in a large group or even mustering the energy to put yourself together and go "grab a coffee" for a casual chat that doesn't seem to be serving an actual purpose, other than connection. But this is the precise type of interaction I'm suggesting, intro-sister. Whether you're intro- or extroverted, social time is essential to your happiness as a human being. Add on the fact that connecting with someone who just *gets* you, understands your stage of life, shares advice or solutions without judgement, listens, and has empathy for whatever it is you're going through... that hour-long coffee may be the very best part of you day, even if you didn't wanna do it in the first place. Trust.

Connecting with people who just "get it" is so important. But that might involve reaching a little further than just the standard best friend circle whom you spend most of your time with. And while we're on the topic of relationships, I want you to know that true, deep, meaningful connection does not require the prerequisite of long-term relationship status. Just because you have a bestie from kindergarten that you still keep in touch with, doesn't mean you can't create meaningful friendships with new people who "get you" later in life and connect in a different way. Maybe kindergarten-best-friend has a completely different lifestyle than you. Maybe she made a choice not to have kids. Maybe she's single and loves it. Maybe she moved away and you've been having a hard time keeping in touch, especially if you're deep in the throes of motherhood and have a shit-load of crap going on at all times, including probably a shit-load of actual crap-smeared baby clothes going into the laundry machine (after you re-wash the stuff that's been sitting there for six days because you forgot to transfer it to the dryer, that is.)

Here's the thing. Often, later in life, friendships blossom with two things. Connection and convenience. There's nothing wrong with admitting your current besties are probably your closest friends due to sheer circumstance. You met a mom at a mom group or program, your kids are the same age, you had a brief connection, found each other on Facebook, decided to have a play date because you live two minutes from one another, and all of the sudden you're going on joint family trips and hanging out every day of your mat leave and comfortably complaining about things your husbands did or didn't do yesterday like she's you're sister.

And with this realization, one day, you might very well find yourself having an internal dialogue quite similar to this one: *"But wait! How can this be? We have only known each other for like a year! Is she my best friend now? What about the aforementioned kindergarten-best-friend? Has this new random friendship somehow overturned our 25-year-long courtship? Do I feel guilty that I don't even know KBF's address these days let alone what she's up to - and I know every single thing there is to know about my new mom-best-friend including how many times she went to the bathroom yesterday? That can't possibly be true! Time is the ultimate indicator of friendship!"*

Time, my friends, is not the ultimate indicator of friendship. I've made some of my very best friends later in life. Just because you were best friends in high school doesn't mean you're guaranteed to be best friends for life. Sorry. That's a tough pill to swallow. We don't always like to admit it, but we absolutely grow apart from people during different stages of our lives. Someone gets married, someone doesn't. Someone decides to move to Australia. Someone has kids. Someone decides against it. Someone works from home. Sometime has a massive corporate job that takes them all over the planet. Someone's into Zumba classes. Someone's into building tiny locomotive replicas in their basement. We are all into different shit, we all go through different life stages at varying times, and we are all allowed to change, evolve and grow as we truly find out who we are as adults.

That means, you and old KBF may not have the same interests anymore. And you may need to release the need to clutch tightly to a 25-year track record when you no longer have a relationship that really serves either of you.

You might have some friends you're hanging onto that you force yourself to hang out with and don't really understand anymore why you even bother. Maybe you drift naturally. That's totally normal and natural.

You might also have some friends who are harder to separate from, but for the sake of you being able to live your life and experience that life with people who get it, you may need to cut the cord with intention, even though you wish them well and there are no hard feelings.

Let's get back to the convenience thing for a hot minute. There is ABSOLUTELY nothing wrong with acquiring bestie-status with someone simply due to convenience. Ever became excellent friends with a colleague at the office because they had a cubicle beside you? (...and were also really cool, cubicle location notwithstanding)? Because why not? You see them every day. You slowly and organically learn things about one another. You start to make inside jokes about the time of day you both need to simultaneously drop a proverbial bomb in the gender-neutral staff bathroom like clockwork. You start sharing what you're doing on the weekends. You introduce each other to your partners at staff holiday parties, and then hang out afterwards and make plans to do it again next weekend. You share intimate details of your relationship and get along so well that senior colleagues start referencing you as the "Bobbsey twins"[14].

*Side bar: my dad allllways used to make this reference when I was hanging with my cousin and we were getting along really well, and until now, I actually had no idea where this reference came from. But it seems to be something the Baby Boomers understand.

You may or may not have built a friendship outside of work if you met under different circumstances, but

---

14   My friend Wikipedia has graciously offered to clear up the long-running confusion about who my Dad has been referencing all these years. "The Bobbsey Twins are the principal characters of what was, for many years, the Stratemeyer Syndicate's longest-running series of American children's novels, penned under the pseudonym Laura Lee Hope. The first of 72 books was published in 1904, the last in 1979, with a separate series of 30 books published from 1987 through 1992. The books related the adventures of the children of the upper-middle-class Bobbsey family, which included two sets of fraternal twins: Nan and Bert, who were 12 years old, and Flossie and Freddie, who were six." Now I'm going to make a donation to Wikipedia because it's a free service and I appreciate their help. You should donate too. (Source: https://en.wikipedia.org/wiki/Bobbsey_Twins)

by nature of environment design, you have no choice but to see each other every day. Maybe you have a lot in common, maybe you don't. But you find things in common because you see each other every damn day and it's hard not to connect dots when you spend that much time together. You do the same job, you have the same frustrations, you understand how frustrating it is when Todd from accounting comes over and close-talks you about the financial reports that are due on Friday, because he has horrible coffee breath and doesn't get the whole boundary thing.

You are connected now. It doesn't have to be with something substantial. And, it doesn't have to be forever, either. Just because you say "I do" to a close friendship during a phase of your life, doesn't mean you're locked in forever. Maybe that colleague example rang true for you when you started your first job out of college, and now you've moved to a different company and have drifted apart. Things happen. A friendship can ignite because you **connect** deeply over a relevant-right-now situation or experience (i.e. having a baby at the same time as someone else and dealing with that shit-storm together); and friendship can ignite due solely to **convenience** and a few minor similarities to start you off (i.e., sharing a cubicle wall with a chick who is also 24, also lives in her parents' basement, and also loves going to Justin Bieber concerts.) Sometimes connection and convenience go together. Sometimes convenience precedes connection. Sometimes connection precedes convenience. Sometimes they stand alone. But if you've made any really great, super close, bestie-level new friendships in your late twenties or early thirties, I'd guess it was probably due to one or the other.

So if you'll allow me to connect the topic of mom-guilt and important relationships for a quick sec, I'd like to wrap this up by saying: please *do not* feel guilty that because your lives are different, you don't feel as connected to your OG friendships as you did a few years ago. If you do, that's great. There's nothing wrong with that either. But if you've been finding yourself in drift-mode for a while and have felt terrible about even the mere thought tiptoeing across your mind that maybe you no longer have things in common anymore... it's all good. Acknowledge that. Give yourself permission to release it. It's not like you have to have an awkward friend break-up meeting at Starbucks or anything; you will just find some comfort in knowing that you will no longer be forcing the continued growth of a relationship that doesn't serve you any longer. You text less, you don't bend over backwards to hang out, and you just keep up with each other on social media. Make no apologies for that. You deserve to find your tribe, and its totes normal for that circle to shift throughout your life.

#MOMFIDENTAF

"True, deep, meaningful connection does not require the prerequisite of a long-term relationship status."

Chapter Sixteen

NAVIGATING MOM-GUILT

Have you ever wanted something really, really bad, but felt guilty about wanting it? Like... wanting to buy a really expensive pair of shoes even though you don't "need them"? Wanting a third piece of chocolate cake even though you've already had two (which, to be clear, is totally fine by me; if you have three slices every night of your life, it might be problematic. But on your Grandpa's 87th birthday? Go for it. Leave the guilt behind. Enjoy it.) Lusting after a particularly good-looking person while you're waiting at the airport for a solo flight, even though you're happily married? Wanting your kid to go back to daycare after a particularly long-long weekend? Being excited that your second child is going into junior kindergarten, but feeling guilty that you're happy about it?

We are predisposed to guilt. I think, actually, if you're a woman and also a mom, you're quite possibly the *most* predisposed to these regularly occurring feelings of guilt. We feel guilty when we're angry or frustrated with our children. We feel guilty that we're happy they're going to a friend's house overnight (HA, HA, BRENDA, THEY'RE ALL YOURS!!! START THE CAR!!!) We feel guilty when we don't spend enough time with our kids. We feel guilty when we want to be alone. We feel guilty that we forgot it was red-shirt-blue-pants-spirit-day at school. We feel guilty if we didn't breastfeed. We feel guilty by association if we were able to breastfeed but our MBF couldn't, and *she* feels guilty. We feel guilty when we're unable to successfully "do it all." We feel guilty if we go back to work. We feel guilty explaining we're "just" a stay at home mom. We feel guilty if we missed that our kid had a fever. We feel guilty that our kids misbehave in public. We feel guilty when we don't feed little Billy a 100% organic, gluten-free, dairy free, vegan, well-balanced meal every damn day. We feel guilty if we don't love every second of motherhood. We feel guilty that we want a break. We feel guilty for feeling guilty. Does that about cover it all? Just kidding, I know that's not even close to all the things we feel guilty for. But for the purpose of keeping this book under eight-hundred-million pages, I'll stop for now.

According to clinical psychotherapist Nicole Grocki, "So-called "mom-guilt" is pervasive among mothers. It can strike at any time and can show itself in any number of "mom" situations. There are enormous expectations from society, media, family and friends about what mothers "should be like" and what we "should do." Should a mom return to work or not? Breastfeed or not? Be happy she is a mom?"[15]

Despite all the apparent reasons we create in our minds to justify feeling bad about doing (or not doing) something, there is really no need for us to feel guilty. When we feel it, it affects nobody else. We feel guilty for leaving the babes alone with their dad for a few nights while we travel, but who does that feeling affect? The hubs? The kids? No, it literally affects only us. And while it's okay to feel a feeling, it's not useful if we just stew about it, feeling horrible, and then returning and having experienced that feeling for no reason at all.

Mom-guilt is definitely a thing. It's a thing as soon as your newborn baby exits your body, and your nurse is immediately telling you how "breast is best!" (with that obnoxious smile, head tilt, and overly upbeat tone, you know the one) and even though you'd already decided you were going to formula feed ahead of time, you feel horrible that someone might be judging your choice or that your poor, poor breasts just can't seem to produce the amount of milk required for nourishment.

---

15   https://www.mindfulreturn.com/mom-guilt/

We feel guilty when we decide to shove a soother in the kid's mouth, just to find some solace in the silence.

We feel guilty when we ask someone to watch the LO for an hour while we go get our hair done, and then we don't even enjoy the much needed and well-deserved time by ourselves.

We feel guilty when the affectionately-named "toddler-hole" will not eat anything on the frickin' planet other than Kraft dinner and chicken nuggets, and we succumb to their tantrums just to ensure they're actually eating *something*. But won't everybody judge me for feeding my kid goldfish crackers instead of celery sticks?

We fucking *always* feel guilty! And we really shouldn't, but I know I'm preaching to the choir when I say… we can't help it. It's natural to feel this way; we were born to be caregivers and when something external threatens that from being perfectly executed by us personally, the byproduct is feeling guilt. (And probably a slew of other things, too.)

It's okay. It's normal. But I do want to help you get over that hump, even if it's just a smidge. The first thing I suggest, if you haven't already, is secure yourself a really good gang of supportive moms with children of similar ages, like I suggested in the previous chapter. That social connection with people who understand what you're going through is truly priceless, I promise.

If you're a new mum, perhaps you've utilized social media to find a local mom-group. That's a great idea. Maybe you and your pre-existing girlfriends somehow managed to get knocked up around the same time, and thus you and your kiddos are going through the same challenges at the same time. Best case scenario. Maybe you have a sister, or a cousin, or an old friend from college who now is pregnant or has a babe at the same stage as yours. HOOK UP WITH HER. (Like, you know, connect with her. Not "hook-up" hook up. Unless that's what you're into.) You'll be amazed at how much you have in common now that you have kids in common. Even if you haven't spoken to Sarah since high school and back then you were frenemies at best. You've grown. You're different people. And now you have a shared interest and can help one another.

Just like any other challenge in this life, going through it with someone who can understand it fully and completely is like winning the lottery of motherhood. Being able to talk it out with Jennifer-from-college who also has a red, bleeding, fucking painful nipple, and is also struggling to get her three-day-old to latch properly, can make a big huge difference in how you feel about it. You may still feel those guilty feelings, but I encourage you to acknowledge them and speak out to your Jennifer-of-choice. (I have a Jennifer of my own, who is actually named Kristen. HI, KRISTEN!

Waves Maybe you don't know it, but connecting with you again after years of unspoken Facebook tab-keeping, when our first babies were 2 months apart, was super helpful for me. You helped me through quite a few things by virtue of simply being 8 weeks ahead of what I was going through. THANKS, GIRL!)

As much as I complain about social media for its own problem-causing issues, it is an excellent and useful tool for finding some mom-babes who are going through the same shit you are. When I was about 23, my parents got divorced. It was heartbreaking and difficult and the topic of many conversations between myself and my sister, bless her heart. We talked until we couldn't talk any more. And those chats were hella helpful, but there was something about connecting with an acquaintance who had gone through divorce recently and was just slightly ahead of me in the process that was incredibly therapeutic. It was like nobody understood me and what I was going through more than this handful of people who had experienced it just before me. I could talk until I was blue in the face to my then boyfriend about it, but he never *quite* understood the pain and emotion I was feeling. I connected to a few people in my friend circle who weren't even my closest buddies, and they were the most helpful conversationalists through that period.

Similarity is comforting. Sharing is therapeutic and while it isn't mandatory that who you share with *must* be going through the same thing you are, it sure as shit is helpful. Mom guilt is just one example of something you go through as a mom that nobody else really understands except other moms. (Well, that and pushing a person out your vagina. Other moms get that, too.) I think just like conquering most other topics mentioned in this book, awareness of your potentially irrational feelings of mom-guilt is the first step. Becoming aware that you are experiencing guilt can be helpful in determining what your next action step can be.

So where does guilt come from, anyway? I'm talking generally to you as a mom, and how the circumstances we've obtained through motherhood dictates higher-than-average feelings of guilt associated with the uniqueness of parenting, but before we qualify guilt specifically as "mom" related, I think it's important to understand guilt at its basic level.

Psychology Today reports that guilt is a "common feeling of emotional distress that signals us when our actions or inactions have caused or might cause harm to another person."[16] So, if you're generally a good person, following all the rules, acting appropriately every day of your life, and then one day you impulse-decide to steal someone's laptop out of their bag at Starbucks, you'll probably feel immense guilt about it afterwards. Your **actions** are pretty much guaranteed to **cause harm** to

16 https://www.psychologytoday.com/ca/blog/the-squeaky-wheel/201411/10-things-you-didnt-know-about-guilt

the person you stole the laptop from. To take it a step further, then, if you **do not** take action to make this better (i.e., return the laptop and apologize, which may not be a perfect solution but would likely clear your conscience) then you're susceptible to *unresolved guilt*, which Psychology Today further describes as "having a snooze alarm in your head that won't shut off." If you're harbouring guilty feelings for stealing that laptop, it's like an internal, annoying alarm going off several times a day, every day, reminding you of what you did, and that makes it really hard to focus or concentrate on anything else. Unresolved guilt makes it hard to think straight and can also impact your productivity, decrease your feelings of joy and contentment, and make it more difficult to enjoy life.

Okay, so knowing what we now know about guilt, let's re-frame this into the "mom" guilt construct. When we feel guilty about things related to motherhood, your actions are garnering guilty feelings about things that aren't *actually* going to cause harm to anyone. It's an exaggerated version of guilt because even though you'd rather Billy not eat those deep-fried chicken fingers, he isn't in any *real* danger or harm if he eats that instead of the carrot sticks and whole grain crackers you'd prefer. It's an exaggerated version of guilt because even though your *action* of taking some much-needed alone time for yourself makes you feel guilty, it does not cause any *real* harm to your children. It's an exaggerated version of guilt because even though your action of returning to work makes you feel guilty, it doesn't cause any *real* harm to your child. Most of the things we feel guilty about are things that do not cause any real harm to our kids. But the thing is, guilt can manifest as "a feeling of responsibility or remorse for an offence, crime, wrongdoing, etc., whether real or imagined."[17] So most of the time, we're sitting there, feeling guilty AF, and it's over something that's not actually real or warranted.

Compound the predisposition to feeling guilt regularly with a) the fact that we often worry that others are judging us and our decisions, and b) the fact that we also often experience feelings of shame as mothers, and you've got a recipe for disaster, mom-style. So not only are we trying to grab hold of some kind of shred of personal confidence and happiness with our physical selves and our postpartum bodies, we now have to navigate building confidence inside our heads with our decisions, our choices, and our discipline strategies as parents. FML.

The main difference between guilt and shame is that guilt generally refers to feelings that you are or will be affecting someone else, and shame generally refers to feelings about ourselves. So when you thought you felt "guilty" about your decision not to breastfeed, it

17 https://www.psychologytoday.com/ca/blog/shame/201305/the-difference-between-guilt-and-shame

may have actually been shame, based on the fact that society shoves "breast is best!" in everyone's faces without any regard for how a mom might feel if she struggles with it. Shame can come from multiple different sources, just like how we've curated our own personal self-image over our entire lives from many different influences.

The bottom line is, guilt at its very core, is the awareness that you've done something wrong and it is derived through our actions. Knowing this, I want you to think again about the last time you felt guilty that you forgot blue-shirt-red-pants-spirit-day. Have you done anything wrong? No. Have you caused harm to anyone? No. Is the world going to end? No. The problem is, as I mentioned previously, there are other factors at play here. It isn't always as simple as, "Okay, Courtney! I'll just not feel guilty anymore! THANKS!" You haven't done anything wrong, but then Susan the secretary points out your mistake in front of a few other moms. Now you likely not only feel guilty, but ashamed and embarrassed, too. Maybe you haven't harmed anyone, but your kid comes home and complains for two hours that *everybody else* had blue shirts and red pants *except them*. So no, you haven't caused harm with your actions, but there are twenty six external sources that are trying their hardest to make sure you *know* you fucked up. But, like, fucking up is inevitable and I'd rather my kid see me make mistakes, regroup, recover, and try again than be perfect all the damn time. An honest mistake or minor error is very different than doing something with intention that has the potential to cause harm (like stealing a laptop) and kids should be able to distinguish that, too. How can they learn the difference if I don't forget shit once in a while? You're welcome, kids.

Being a mom is hard. Fucking hard, actually, if you'll recall. My advice for getting over mom-guilt is to reinforce the fact that you are a goddamn human and you simply cannot satisfy everyone; your kids, your spouse, and Susan the secretary included. But if there's one thing I know for sure, it's that you try your damn hardest. Of course, you do! Every single mom on this earth, every mom in the audience at the Christmas concert, every mom in the waiting room at gymnastics... every mom is just out there doing her very best every single day. I'm looking at you - yes, you! Reading this book! - I know, to my core, that all you want to do is provide the best possible life for your kids and be the most loving, supportive, caring, and stable parent that you can be. There isn't a doubt in my mind. Breathe that in for a minute. You are an incredible parent. You are an incredible parent. **YOU ARE AN AMAZING MOM.** Look at you, reading this book so you can learn how to be a mom who is CONFIDENT AS FUCK. You know who that benefits? Everyone else in your life. Literally. You care so much about other people that you want to best your damn self so that everybody else benefits. You are selfless and giving and put everybody else before yourself. I can (almost) guarantee that. But you know what, honey? You aren't nearly as good for your family if you are constantly depleted, exhausted, bat-shit-guilty and a self-loathing sulk all the time.

Your parenting decisions are the ones you must make for **you**. Maybe you go back to work for your own sanity, for financial reasons, or because you just really love your job and had a great career before kids, and you shouldn't have to sacrifice that. Maybe you want to go back for the sole purpose to having adult time because you crave it. That's okay to admit! Maybe your work is so valuable to you and gives you another sense of purpose, along with being a caregiver. I don't actually care what your reason is, and it should not matter what anybody else thinks, remember? Part of becoming your own personal and unique brand of MOMFIDENT AS F*CK is learning how to be confident in your decisions, and with that comes the release of guilt. At least a little bit, to start. When you are so sure that giving back to yourself (via alone time, or a solo trip, or going back to work, or having grandma watch the kids for a weekend) is just as, if not MORE important than mothering your children, you will be better equipped to feel good about that decision. Yes, I said more important than mothering. Because you can't be a high-level, self-loving, body-accepting, kickass mom if you aren't first taking damn good care of yourself, your mental health and your sanity. Then, after you drop those kiddos off with G-ma, you can just experience the feeling of missing your kids, instead of feeling like you're slighting them somehow. Because you're not.

Now, of course, I'm not suggesting that you will never experience guilt in your life. It's a normal feeling and we all experience it, even outside of feeling it in relation to being a mom. I am, however, suggesting that most of us are 100% exaggerating the amount of guilt we feel as moms and often it isn't even for a legitimate reason. So I want you to evaluate your own feelings the next time they come up. Are you feeling guilty because your actions are *actually* causing your children harm? I think at least 90% of the time, the answer is no. If that's the case, try to release that guilt. If the first step is becoming aware of it, the second step is to determine if you have actually done anything wrong that causes harm.

Another thing you can do when you catch yourself feeling guilty, after you've acknowledge it and determined that you aren't actually causing anyone harm, is to remind yourself of WHY you're doing the action you're doing, that's making you feel guilty. It could look like this: if you're feeling guilty because you sent your kid to his room for a time out, ask yourself if you're causing anyone legitimate harm with your action (sending your kid to his room.) No. Billy is fine, and furthermore, deserves to be in there; he just sucker punched you in the boob because he didn't like what you gave him for breakfast. He's fine, despite having a screaming fit that sounds like a rhinoceros is being brutally murdered in his bedroom. Now ask yourself why you're taking the action you're taking. You've sent him to his room because he was misbehaving. He was inappropriately physical and he needs to be disciplined so he grows up to be a decent human who understands consequences and doesn't punch people in the boob or become a Starbucks laptop stealer. This technique can help you because, with all the rhinoceros-like antics going on, it can get really tempting to just give in and let him out of his room so you don't have to listen to it anymore. But by justifying *why* you're taking the action, that isn't causing any real harm, even though you feel guilty... you're better able to stick with it. Try not to let the guilt and the easy-way-out dictate your next moves. If you find yourself in a pattern of succumbing to every waking need, request, and desire of your children so as to not upset them, you may be employing guilt in an unhealthy way. Your kids need to experience being away from you. Your kids need discipline. Your kids are going to be fine if you're a working mom. Your kids are going to be fine whether you breastfeed them or not. Your kids are going to be fine if they have to go to their room for a time out. Your kids are going to be fine at Grandma's for the weekend. Your kids are going to be fine if they eat chicken nuggets for dinner. I think we should all get matching tattoos that say "they're going to be fine."

Sometimes our guilt comes from severe expectation dysmorphia. I think I just made that term up. Basically, I'm saying that if you have expectations for things to go one way, and then they don't... you may be left feeling guilty about it. Oh, you expected your family photos to go smoothly? HA! Now you're feeling guilty (and probably embarrassed, frustrated, angry...) that the poor photographer has to deal with your real-life shitshow for 30 minutes. Actually, I don't think I even need to explain different scenarios where your guilt may be heightened; I'm pretty sure we all create guilt around literally anything to do with being a mom.

Please find comfort in knowing that we all experience this shit. Now promptly cut that shit out and start evaluating: am I actually hurting anyone? 99% of the time, I'm sure your answer will be no. Now go get your hair cut and enjoy yourself. They're going to be fine.

#MOMFIDENTAF

"You aren't good for anybody if you are constantly depleted, exhausted, bat-shit-guilty and a self-loathing sulk 24/7."

Chapter Seventeen

ROSE COLOURED SELF-IMAGE

Well, it looks like this might be the end. Is it really the end, though? No. Not really. Like I said, this whole *MOMFIDENT AS F*CK* thing is really an extremely personal and individual journey, a unique process, and not at all a destination. You will need to circle back now and again. You will face new challenges that require you to do some more hard work. Or maybe, some *heart* work. You will need to return to the practice of treating yourself nicer if you find that you're regularly shit-thinking again. The important part is that you become aware of how you think and speak about yourself, and do the work to get back to a kinder place.

If you'll allow me to give you a really weird yet well-rounded example of looking at yourself with a better lens on a regular basis, I want you to imagine for a second the last time you were house shopping. Yes, house shopping. Do you remember the last time you were in the process of finding the perfect place for you? Maybe you were trying to find your forever home; moving somewhere bigger after you had a family, or even finding the perfect rental in the heart of a flourishing downtown environment (and I know that can take YEARS). Remember when you found a place you absolutely LOVED? Remember how you looked at it with rose-coloured glasses, with opportunity, with ideas and plans, with "yeah but we can just renovate that" sentiment? Remember how beautiful it looked, how well it was staged, how much storage space it had? Remember how much better the kitchen flowed and how much family space there was? And then, after the place closes and you're in there, it feels like a dream. You love your new place and you are ecstatic to have visitors and show them around. You decorate to your liking and you live for those Sunday nights with a candle, a clean kitchen, a glass of wine and an episode of *Friends*.

But then… the honeymoon phase wears off. This could take a year or five, but things start getting a little messy; life happens; maybe the family expands again… and suddenly the place you were once obsessed with seems to have more cons than pros. Why is that corner cabinet in your kitchen so poorly organized? How come there isn't any more space in that massive closet? How'd all the corners of the walls get chipped like that? Why is the hardwood floor so scratched up? This main floor layout is *so annoying*. If we had the money, we'd do a whole renovation of this laundry room. I want to add a deck to the backyard but it's such an awkward space. Who put that island there? If we had a bigger space we'd entertain more. I really wish we'd found a place with an elevator and not a third-floor walk-up. Suddenly, the honeymoon's over and you start becoming less opportunistic and more critical. You highlight flaws and forget about benefits. You are more focused on what you *don't* like than what you *do* like. If other people compliment you on a feature of the house, you deflect it. You suddenly believe the grass is greener and start looking for somewhere new to live again, even if it's just to fantasize about places that are way out of your budget but appear to be "perfect" in the pictures. You stop loving the place you were once thrilled with. You let go of the love and focus only on the hate, and then the hate grows because you don't stop to think about how well this place actually serves you. You can't see opportunity anymore, not like that first time you came to the open house. You are too comfortable and it's become easier to be critical than satisfied.

This is what we do to ourselves. Isn't it? There's a certain point in your life when you are fully, completely, and 100% satisfied with yourself 24/7. You never think about the "negative" traits you have, and you think nothing but positive or neutral thoughts about yourself at all times. You're just going along, living your life, without insecurities, doubts, worries, fears, or any lack of confidence. **This was you as a child.** We're all like this as children. I can see it in my daughter and I'm sure you can recognize this in your own children. But there comes a point in life where we start to notice what's going on around us, and suddenly we aren't so satisfied with ourselves. Over time, if we don't become aware of it, that dissatisfaction grows and grows, and we feed it with negative self-talk, negative thinking, and beating ourselves up about things we don't have, instead of feeling good about the things we do have. **What you focus on, expands.** So, as you continue thinking all these things about how you don't like X about yourself, all the way through elementary school, middle school, and high school, with all that negative shit swirling around you at all times, the negative mindset expands. We don't talk about it though, we all just go on through life silently suffering, quietly thinking we're less than, unworthy, not capable, unfit, not enough, and struggling through our class presentations because we're afraid of what people might think of us if we put ourselves out there. If someone gives you a compliment, you deflect it, because why on earth would anybody recognize anything good about you? *You stop loving the place you were once thrilled with. You let go of the love and focus only on the hate, and then the hate grows because you don't stop yourself to think about how well this place actually serves you. You can't see opportunity anymore. You are too comfortable and it's become easier to be critical than satisfied.* Sound familiar? (I hope it does because that's literally a direct quote from the end of the paragraph about your love for your house fading.)

It's easy to fall into default mode. The question is, what does your default mode look like? What's the kind of stuff that floats around in your head on a regular basis? What you focus on, you will feel. Unfortunately, all kinds of moments, experiences, and external influences like unkind people, advertising, and society's perpetual highlight of only one body type, have slowly, over time, made you doubt yourself and whether you measure up. Imagine how you feel about your own children. When they're born, you look at them in awe and wonder how something so perfect could be real. You are mesmerized and have so many great hopes and dreams for this tiny miracle human. Then, the toddler years arrive and you might have a few other feelings (LOL), but you still have so much love and gratitude for being able to carry and birth this human, and watch them grow up. If that beautiful soul came to you and told you about how something or someone was getting them down, making them feel less-than, and holding them back from being confident, fulfilled, and happy... you'd likely go into mama-bear mode and want to take whoever was responsible to the nearest fight club, #amiright? When something threatens your child's sense of self, self-esteem, happiness, confidence, and self-acceptance, you couldn't be more furious. You look at your child and you see the big picture; you see their heart, their personality, their traits, you see them as a whole, incredible person. Yet, when you look at yourself, you see something that you want to change, mold, fit into a skinny box and make sure appealing to the culturally accepted body and beauty ideals is a big check mark off life's to-do list. We've been knocked down so many times, and allow our self-worth to crumble, but we couldn't fathom this happening to our own children. The truth is though, your kids look back at you with the same loving potential and non-judgemental gaze as you do them. You're the only thing that matters to them (and well, I guess Dad too...) and they love every inch of you, whether you're a size 2 or a size 22. It's not selfish or conceited or ego-driven to look at yourself with the same love-filled lens that others do. It's important, priority work learning to re-accept and love yourself, and get back to a place where acceptance comes with ease and flow, you have less difficult change room moments and you don't even stop for a second to hesitate before dropping your towel and flitting to the beach in your bathing suit, without caring if a single person is watching you strut.

Re-imagine what ideal looks like. Let go of trying to squish yourself into the exact frame of a photoshopped magazine model. Know that 99% of the world has cellulite and despite what society and advertising and that one chick from high school who regularly PMs you on Facebook messenger about her "opportunity" might say...

YOU CAN LIVE A BRILLIANT LIFE WITH CELLULITE. *GASP*

YOU CAN BE SUCCESSFUL AND VALUABLE WITH FAT ON YOUR BODY.

YOU HAVE MORE TO CONTRIBUTE TO THE WORLD THAN THE SIZE OF YOUR PANTS.

There, I'm so glad I got that off my chest. And, no, thank you, Brittany, I don't need any cellulite cream. No, no, please don't circle back in a few months to "check in." Thanks.

Re-define ideal. What if "ideal" was exactly what your body looks like *right now*? How good and delicious and satisfying would that feel? As we established earlier, that doesn't mean you can't desire change for that body, especially if you've taken stock of your lifestyle and realize you're not eating well and aren't moving regularly. If you start making healthy changes, your body is likely to change, too. But what I really want you to remember, is to focus on appreciation and trust and acceptance of your body **no matter what size**. That means right now, sister. When you practice a love for yourself and body *first*, you are less likely to put so much of your worth in the successful (or unsuccessful) shedding of X amount of pounds. You're unlikely to be sitting around, waiting until circumstances are perfect before you decide that yes, I *do* accept myself and *now* I feel good in my skin. Don't wait. Start now. It's like a savings account. You need to start making self-love deposits on a regular, consistent basis, if you want your self-worth account to amount to anything in the future, just like you would if you wanted to build actual money in a bank account. Don't sit around complaining about how you don't have a lot of savings yet, if you don't do the hard work to progress towards those savings. Savings accrues by virtue of tiny, seemingly irrelevant but massively important deposits over time, with consistency. Don't allow yourself to think you're somehow "less than" because you don't have a big lump sum of money in your account to be proud of; be proud now for making forward steps and appreciating where you are. And, most importantly, don't you dare expect to wake up tomorrow with $500,000 if you don't start dropping regular cash into that account with purpose and intention *right now*. The best time to start is now.

"*We are what we repeatedly do. Excellence, then, is not an act but a habit.*" —Will Durant

***

About a year after publishing my first project, the *#MOMFIDENT AF Self-Love Journal*, I wound up with a bad review on Amazon and I took it kind of personally. I shouldn't have. It wasn't a complaint against me personally, but it was my first book and my first review that wasn't 5 stars, and I didn't feel it was fair. The customer was disappointed that the pages inside the journal ask the same questions every single day. I mention this particular review because it was the first time I realized that not everybody understands what it takes to truly change how your own self-image functions. This person's opinion brought up a great point about consistency and how our self-image can be impacted heavily by consistency... of action or inaction. Yes, all the pages in the 90-day journal are the same 6 journal prompts, but there is reason for this. It's repetitive on purpose. (And also, there are example pages you can view if you want to look before you buy, so...) Consistency is important when it comes to changing the way you think about yourself and your circumstances, just like consistency is important when it comes to movement, savings, brushing your teeth, and getting oil changes, obviously. With regular focus on some key aspects, you can start to shift those things. For example, one of the prompts in the journal asks you to list what you're grateful for today. I probably don't need to educate you on the benefits of gratitude, but when implemented regularly, it can be completely life-changing.

Regularly practicing gratitude, stating things you're grateful for, and consistently writing them down, has been scientifically shown to improve psychological health and well-being. Bringing awareness to the good things in your life can proactively shift the mindset to one more conducive to positivity, openness, happiness and fulfillment. A study published in the *Journal of Applied Sport Psychology* found that "gratitude increased athletes' self-esteem" and "reduces social comparisons. Rather than becoming resentful toward people who have more money or better jobs—a major factor in reduced self-esteem—grateful people are able to appreciate other people's accomplishments."[18]

If you do a gratitude list one day and then forget to do it again, you aren't likely to reap many benefits. But if you can list something every day on a regular basis? You will not believe the difference it can make for you. If you've never done it before you might be skeptical. All I can say is **try it**.

---

18 Amy Morin, "7 Scientifically Proven Benefits of Gratitude," Psychology Today (April 2015): psychologytoday.com/ca/blog/what-mentally-strong-people-dont-do/201504/7-scientifically-proven-benefits-gratitude

Similarly, one of the journal prompts asks you to list something you love about yourself right now. Time and time again, the feedback from my journal-users remains: that question takes them the longest to answer at first, and they sit thinking and wondering what to write for a few minutes every time. This journal is meant to be done in under five minutes each day, so you can see how this delay can waste unnecessary time. But something magical happens when you continue pushing yourself through this kind of uncomfortable piece of the journal for a few weeks. Suddenly, you start thinking of things you love about yourself much easier. You start thinking of them proactively, actually, instead of reactively. That means, you start realizing things you love about yourself in advance, and your thought is followed closely by "I'm gonna put that in my journal for tomorrow." The same thing happens with gratitude. You are able to start being proactive about how you feel about yourself and your life, instead of reacting and struggling to come up with an answer. Suddenly, as you bend down to pick up your kids and realize you're strong as heck and can carry both of them up a full flight of stairs without blinking an eye, you realize you're grateful for how strong your body is. Not because it has a six-pack, but because it is powerful beyond measure, size excluded. That could fall under gratitude or something you love about yourself, but the important part is this: you noticed it. Before, you would have just carried on with your day. But, with regular and consistent energy spent on gratitude and self-love, you become aware of more of the awesome shit, proactively. Then you solidify it by writing it physically into your journal. Now you have a tangible record of all kinds of shit you love about yourself, and are grateful for. Win-win, no?

Habits are important for building a life you love, a self you accept, a body you embrace and relationships that thrive. Habits are built on consistency, and consistency of action can be highly beneficial to you, especially as it relates to the way you think and speak about yourself. If you have a poor self image, chances are you are consistently allowing negative thoughts and words about yourself permeate every fiber of your being. If you want to consistently sit back and allow that to happen, that's your prerogative. If you want to consistently choose not to give a 90-day journal more than just a three day try, that's up to you. If you're willing to take consistent action towards shaping your default mode, it will change. Drastically.

If you're in the regular habit of having coffee with your best friend every week, chances are you are well-connected and know exactly what each other are up to. Skip the date and wind up missing it for months on end? Chances are you have not a clue what's going on in her life and your relationship isn't the same as it would be if you kept in touch regularly. That's a habit that benefits you.

If you're in the regular habit of spending 30 minutes every other day moving your body intentionally, chances are that you're feeling good in your body, you're getting stronger and get less out of breath when you are forced to take the stairs at work because the elevator is broken. Skip the movement sessions and wind up ditching them for a few months? Chances are your fitness level will slide, your cardiovascular capacity will shift, and you'll be sweating like a mo-fo instead of gliding up the stairs with ease. That's a habit that benefits you.

If you're in the regular habit of writing 500 words every morning, chances are high that you'll be finished that book in no time. Stop writing regularly because of the snooze button? Chances are that book won't get finished, and you'll be scratching your head with regret instead of spreading the word about your book launch next month. That's a habit that benefits you.

We are what we repeatedly do. So if you're repeatedly shit talking yourself, letting yourself believe that you aren't worthy, or focusing only on the negative things going on in your life, there's no way forward. You'll be eating negative Nancy sandwiches for the rest of your life, if you don't make a change. The question is, will you do what's necessary to generate the change needed to embrace your life?

#MOMFIDENTAF

"Start making self-love deposits on a regular, consistent basis, if you want your self-worth account to amount to anything in the future."

Last Word

As I sit down to write what will be known as the "conclusion" of this book, I've just come in the door after walking my four-year-old to school the morning after our first big snowstorm of Canadian winter 2019. She wanted to walk, so I obliged. We were decked head to toe in snow gear, she did a snow angel on the front lawn (with her backpack on...), and then approximately three minutes after leaving our house she was complaining and dragging behind me and telling me she can't walk. *Rolls eyes*. On the way back, as I'm casually strutting down a semi-steep hill making my way back home, a man who is parallel parked on said hill looks over and says in a sarcastic tone:

"Isn't this weather great?" I'm pretty sure he rolled his eyes for punctuation, but it was hard to tell. He had what looked like a spring jacket on, no hat, no gloves, running shoes, and was trying to scrape the accumulated ice off his back windshield.

"Yeah!" I said, "I actually love winter!" I pretended not to notice his sarcastic tone. He scoffed.

He continued: "I love it about as much as I love poking myself in the eye with a needle!"

I laughed to indicate I was answering lightheartedly and that I wasn't looking for an argument - we could agree to disagree. But I couldn't help but think on the rest of my way home: things are good or bad based on how you choose to look at them. Here's what I know: I live in Canada. At least six months of the year are cold and snowy. There's no way around it. I can choose to be miserable for six months, complain about the weather like there's any possible way for me to impact it changing, dress poorly for the elements like I didn't know it was coming, struggle through scraping ice off my window with frozen extremities, get soaked calves-down from wearing inappropriate footwear and then try to encourage passersby to join me in my misery. Or, I can realize that winter is coming whether I like it or not, prepare with proper clothing, and enjoy the beauty of it even though it's slightly annoying dragging a kindergartener through it to get to school. Do you see the difference?

If you don't like the circumstances, there is absolutely no benefit to just complaining about them but not doing anything to change the proverbial climate.

If you despise the weather so much where you live, so much so that you'd rather poke your eyeballs out than deal with it, THEN MOVE. There are places in Canada that don't get hit as hard with winter weather. Oh, you can't move because all your family is in this town, right here, right where it's apparently eyeball-stabbingly terrible? THEN ADJUST. Get yourself a damn winter coat. Invest in high quality winter footwear. Wear a hat and gloves, or a balaclava for all I care, but for God's sake, **dress appropriately.** If you are prepared for winter, you won't be as bothered by it. You just know it takes longer to prepare to go somewhere, (especially if you have a kindergartener.) There's nothing worse than someone complaining but not taking action to move towards something better, even a little bit better. Even 5/10 instead of 2/10. ADJUST.

I learned while working at a General Motors through a few summers in University that you have the power to choose your attitude at all times, and you're literally the only one who has the ability to do it. I used to work double shifts, overnights, literally any job that required coverage I'd do, because it was incredible money for a University student and, like, what the hell else did I have going on? I worked with people of all ages, classes, and education levels. I worked as a partner to basically a different person every week. Most people were miserable. These people were miserable during eight hours of their *permanent*, well-paying jobs. This was what they were doing to make a living, to support their families, to pay the bills. And they hated it. I understand it's not always as simple as just saying, "if you're miserable, get a new job then!", because things are more complicated than that. But one day, a few weeks in, I started working with a man who had the most upbeat, positive attitude. He sang along to the radio all day long, asked me questions about myself, made jokes, chatted with everyone, and skipped his way in to work. I decided to ask him about it, because he was really obviously an anomaly in this place.

"Well, I have to be here for eight hours," he said. "That's a lot of time in my life that I spend in this place. I choose to enjoy myself for eight hours, because if I have to be here, I might as well choose to be happy about it, right?"

MOTHER FUCKING RIGHT.

You can choose. You can make a conscious choice to reject society's standards, reject the pressure to "fit" a certain mold, reject the idea that any kind of perfection exists, and look at yourself with new, soft, welcoming eyes.

You can choose to be grateful for what you have in your life, instead of frustrated for what you don't have.

You can choose to see the beauty in your imperfections; to let go of trying obsessively to be a specific weight or size; to spend any more time caring that you have a belly full of stretch marks, cellulite on your ass, or are thirty pounds heavier than you were before pre-baby.

You can choose to focus on the things you love about yourself, release the things you don't, and over time build a consistent positive habit that truly has the power to change what you think on default mode.

You can choose. You *get* to choose. Are you going to be miserable about a season that you don't enjoy, or try to see the good in winter? Are you going to suffer through eight hours of your day, or realize that you might as well find some joy for yourself, instead of hating every minute? Are you going to be in a constant state of misery about yourself, because you aren't "where you want to be" right now, or realize that embracing your *now* is literally the first and most important step, if you desire change at all?

You can do this. I promise. It starts with you and as you progress over the next few months of your journey, you're going to find your own version of living a life that can only be described as…

MOMFIDENT AS F*CK.

You've got this, babe. It's time to start shifting.

#MOMFIDENTAF

"Just do what you want and be prepared that not everybody will understand. Fuck them, anyway. How's that for an inspirational quote? 🖕"

About the Author

Courtney St Croix is a 4x Best-Selling Author, Top-Rated Podcast Host, Mindset Transformation Coach, and CEO of boutique publishing house MOMFIDENT AF Media. In 2015, Courtney set out on a personal journey to whole-body self-acceptance, as she recovered from the  ultimate female body transformation experience of pre- and post-pregnancy.

Through a long-time struggle with a lack of both confidence and a healthy body image, Courtney wanted to figure out how to create and foster a more confident and self-assured mindset. After becoming a certified Life Purpose and Confidence Coach, she now understands where true confidence is conceived, and aims to share the truths of self-love and self-acceptance with women on a daily basis.

Courtney created the Best-Selling "#MomfidentAF Self-Love Journal" in 2018, a similar journal for adolescent girls in 2019, and has since published two other works dedicated to helping women learn to embrace their now and evolve to new levels. She leads group authorship projects through MOMFIDENT AF Media to allow women to share their own stories of self-love, and chats about confidence and motherhood on her top-rated show, The Momfidence Podcast.

Courtney lives in Ontario, Canada with her husband Chris, daughter Presley and colossal dog, Molson.

MORE MOMFIDENT AF

Find more information, projects, The Momfident Podcast and coaching resources at
GetMomfidentAF.com

Manufactured by Amazon.ca
Bolton, ON